Pierogi

A Delicious Collection of Tasty Pierogi Recipes

By
BookSumo Press

Published by
http://www.booksumo.com

ENJOY THE RECIPES?

KEEP ON COOKING
WITH 6 MORE FREE COOKBOOKS!

Visit our website and simply enter your email address to join the club and receive your 6 cookbooks.

http://booksumo.com/magnet

https://www.instagram.com/booksumopress/

https://www.facebook.com/booksumo/

LEGAL NOTES

Table of Contents

How to Make a Pierogi

Prep Time: 30 mins
Total Time: 1 hr

Servings per Recipe: 1
Calories	41.5
Fat	1.0g
Cholesterol	14.4mg
Sodium	49.7mg
Carbohydrates	6.4g
Protein	1.3g

Ingredients

2 large eggs
1/2 tsp salt
2 C. flour
2 oz. cream cheese
water
mashed potatoes

sautéed onion
sour cream

Directions

1. Get a food blender: Place in it the salt and four then combine them well.
2. Combine in the eggs with cream cheese then blend them for 22 sec. add the water gradually until you get a ball of dough.
3. Place the dough ball on a floured surface and cover it with a towel. Let it sit for 22 min.
4. Place half of the dough on a floured surface until it becomes 1/16 inches thick.
5. Use a 5 inches cookie cutter to cut the dough into circles. Place 2 tbsp of the potato mix on one side of a dough circle.
6. Pull the other half of dough over it to cover it then press it with a fork to seal it.
7. Repeat the process with the remaining dough.
8. Bring a large pot of water to a boil. Place in it some pierogies with olive oil and let them cook for 3 to 4 min.
9. Drain them and place them aside then cook the remaining pierogies.
10. Gently stir the pierogies with butter, onion, a pinch of salt and pepper then serve them right away.
11. Enjoy.

OFF-CAMPUS
Pierogies

Prep Time: 10 mins
Total Time: 25 mins

Servings per Recipe: 6
Calories	319.6
Fat	24.5g
Cholesterol	49.8mg
Sodium	755.5mg
Carbohydrates	14.3g
Protein	11.6g

Ingredients
2 medium onions, chopped
2 tbsp margarine
1 head cabbage, chopped
1 lb turkey kielbasa, sliced
33 oz. potato & cheese pierogies
1 dash pepper

Directions
1. Place a large pan over medium heat: Heat in it the butter. Add the onion and cook it for 3 min.
2. Stir in the cabbage with a pinch of salt. Put on the lid and let them cook for 12 min over low heat.
3. Stir the kielbasa into the cabbage mix. Put on the lid and let them cook for an extra 12 min.
4. Prepare the pierogies by following the instructions on the package.
5. Once they are done, stir the pierogies into the kielbasa pan and cook them for an extra 6 min. serve them hot.
6. Enjoy.

Party
Pierogies

Prep Time: 20 mins
Total Time: 3 hr 20 mins

Servings per Recipe: 16
Calories   105.5
Fat   11.5g
Cholesterol   30.5mg
Sodium   1.9mg
Carbohydrates   0.8g
Protein   0.2g

Ingredients
48 pierogies
1 C. unsalted butter, melted
1 large white onion, chopped
salt
pepper

Directions
1. Lay the pierogies in a crock pot and place it aside.
2. Place a heavy saucepan over medium heat. Heat in it the butter then cook in it the onion for 6 min.
3. Pour the onion all over the pierogies then season them with some salt and pepper.
4. Put on the lid and let them cook for 3 h on high.
5. Once the time is up, serve them hot.
6. Enjoy.

EUROPEAN
Pierogies

Prep Time: 30 mins
Total Time: 45 mins

Servings per Recipe: 6
Calories	60.2
Fat	0.9g
Cholesterol	6.1mg
Sodium	19.6mg
Carbohydrates	10.7g
Protein	2.0g

Ingredients
4 C. all-purpose flour
1 C. water
1 large egg
3 C. instant mashed potatoes, cooked
4 -6 oz. cheddar cheese
1 small onion, chopped and sautéed
salt and pepper

Directions
1. Get a large mixing bowl: Pour in it 4 C. of flour then make a small hole in the center for it.
2. Place in it the egg with water and a pinch of salt. Mix them well until you get a smooth dough.
3. Get a mixing bowl: Mix in it the mashed potato with cheese, onion, a pinch of salt and pepper.
4. Add 2 tsp of the potato mix to the dough and mix them well.
5. Place the dough on floured surface and flatten it until it becomes 1/8 inches thick.
6. Use a 3 to 4 inches cookie cutter to cut the dough into circles.
7. Put 1 tbsp of the filling on the side of one circle then fold the other half of dough over it to cover it.
8. Press the edges with a fork to seal them.
9. Bring a large pot of water to a boil. Place in it the pierogies and cook them until they rise on top.
10. Drain the pierogies from the hot water then serve them with your favorite sauce.
11. Enjoy.

Hungarian
Casserole

Prep Time: 30 mins
Total Time: 1 hr 15 mins

Servings per Recipe: 8
Calories   570.7
Fat   105.4mg
Cholesterol   939.3mg
Sodium   73.7g
Carbohydrates   20.7g
Protein   21.5g

Ingredients

16 oz. wide egg noodles
6 C. prepared mashed potatoes
1/4 C. butter
2 large onions, chopped
garlic, minced
1 1/2 C. shredded cheddar cheese

1 1/2 C. shredded white processed cheese
sour cream

Directions

1. Before you do anything, preheat the oven to 350 F. Grease it with some butter.
2. Prepare the noodles by following the instructions on the package and cook them until they become dente.
3. Place a large pan over medium heat: Heat in it the butter. Cook in it the onion with garlic for 2 min.
4. Get a large mixing bowl: Mix in it the potato with onion mix, a pinch of salt and pepper.
5. Place half of the cooked noodles in a greased casserole dish. Spread over it the potato and onion mix.
6. Sprinkle the cheddar cheese on top then lay over it the remaining noodles.
7. Sprinkle the American cheese on top. Place the casserole in the oven and let it cook for 35 to 45 min. Serve it hot.
8. Enjoy.

TRADITIONAL
Sauerkraut
Pierogies

Prep Time: 10 mins
Total Time: 30 mins

Servings per Recipe: 4	
Calories	364.9
Fat	5.5g
Cholesterol	49.6mg
Sodium	1021.2mg
Carbohydrates	67.0g
Protein	11.0g

Ingredients
3 C. sauerkraut, chopped
1 medium chopped onion
4 tbsp vegetable shortening
2 tbsp sour cream
salt and pepper
2 1/2 C. flour
1/2 tsp salt

1 egg
2 tsp oil
3/4 C. warm water

Directions
1. To make the filling:
2. Place a large pan over medium heat: Melt the shortening in it. Sauté in it the onion for 3 min.
3. Stir in the sauerkraut with cream, a pinch of salt and pepper. Lower the heat and let them cook for 16 min.
4. Once the time is up, place the filling aside to cool down completely.
5. To make the dough:
6. Get a large mixing bowl: Mix in it the flour with salt, oil, egg and water. Combine them well until your get a dough.
7. Place the dough on a floured surface and knead it for few minutes until it becomes soft.
8. Divide the dough into pieces and wrap them in a paper towels. Place them aside to rise for 10 to 12 min.
9. Roll the dough on a floured surface and cut into circles with a cookie cutter.
10. Put 1 tbsp of the filling on one side of the dough circle then fold the other half over it.
11. Wet the dough circle edges with some water then press them with a fork to seal them.
12. Bring a large salted pot of water to a boil. Place in it some pierogies then cook them until they rise on top.
13. Drain them and place them in a serving plate. Drizzle over them some melted butter and repeat the process with the remaining pierogies.
14. Serve your pierogies warm with your favorite dipping sauce.
15. Enjoy.

Southwest
Pierogies

Prep Time: 30 mins

Total Time: 1 hr

Servings per Recipe: 6

Calories	561.4
Fat	33.3g
Cholesterol	153.2mg
Sodium	710.9mg
Carbohydrates	40.6g
Protein	25.5g

Ingredients

2 C. flour
1 egg, whisked
1/2 tsp salt
1/4 C. butter, cubed
1/2 C. sour cream
1 lb ground turkey
1/2 C. finely diced onion
2 minced garlic cloves
1/4 C. corn kernel
3 chipotle peppers, minced
2 tbsp of the adobo sauce
1/4 tsp salt

1/2 tsp paprika
1/4 tsp cumin
1/4 tsp cayenne
1 C. chicken stock
2 C. Simply Potatoes Traditional Mashed Potatoes
1/2 C. colby-monterey jack cheese
2 - 3 tbsp melted butter
1 C. sour cream
3 tbsp taco seasoning
1 tbsp chopped green onion

Directions

1. To prepare the dough:
2. Get a food blender: Combine in it the flour with salt. Mix in the beaten egg until they become coarse.
3. Pour in it the sour cream with butter then pulse them several times until they become smooth.
4. Pour the mix into a floured surface and shape it into a ball. Cover it with a paper towel and let it rest for 22 min.
5. To make the filling:
6. Get a large mixing bowl: Mix in it the potato with cheese, a pinch of salt and pepper. Place it aside.
7. Place the dough on a floured surface. Use a cookie cutter to cut it into circles.
8. Place 1 tbsp of the filling on the side of the dough then fold the other half over it.
9. Wet the dough edges with some water then press them with a fork to seal them.

10. Place a large pan over medium heat. Melt in it some butter. Add to it the pierogies and cook them for 1 to 2 min on each side.
11. Get a small mixing bowl: Whisk in it the sour cream, chopped green onion, taco seasoning, a pinch of salt and pepper to make the sauce.
12. Serve your pierogies with the taco sauce.
13. Enjoy.

Potato Pierogies
on a Spring Bed

Prep Time: 10 mins
Total Time: 35 mins

Servings per Recipe: 3
Calories	833.7
Fat	72.2g
Cholesterol	181.0mg
Sodium	1691.8mg
Carbohydrates	26.4g
Protein	23.2g

Ingredients
12 frozen potato and onion pierogies
8 tbsp butter
1 large onion, chopped
1 head cabbage, chopped
salt and pepper
1 lb turkey kielbasa, coins

Directions
1. Place a large salted pot of water over high heat. Bring it to a boil.
2. Cook in it the pierogies in batches for 6 to 8.
3. Place a large pan over medium heat. Heat the butter in it. Cook in it the onion with a pinch of salt for 4 min.
4. Stir in the cabbage with a pinch of salt and pepper. Cook them for 4 to 6 min.
5. Mix in it kielbasa then lower the heat. Place the pierogies on top and season them with some salt and pepper.
6. Place some of the cabbage mix over the pierogies then serve them warm.
7. Enjoy.

PIEROGI
Pan

Prep Time: 5 mins
Total Time: 25 mins

Servings per Recipe: 4
Calories   92.5
Fat   9.7g
Cholesterol   26.2mg
Sodium   118.6mg
Carbohydrates   0.1g
Protein   1.5g

Ingredients
1 box frozen potato & cheese pierogi
3 tbsp grated parmesan cheese
3 tbsp butter, melted

Directions
1. Before you do anything, preheat the oven to 425 F. Grease a casserole dish with some butter.
2. Bring a large pot of salted water to a boil. Cook in it the pierogies for 4 to 5 min.
3. Remove the pierogies from the water and place them in the casserole dish.
4. Drizzle the butter on top then cover them with parmesan cheese.
5. Place the casserole in the oven and let it cook for 16 to 22 min until it becomes golden. Serve it hot.
6. Enjoy.

Full
German Dinner

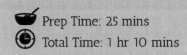

Prep Time: 25 mins
Total Time: 1 hr 10 mins

Servings per Recipe: 16
Calories   478.5
Fat   26.6g
Cholesterol   99.3mg
Sodium   669.1mg
Carbohydrates   46.1g
Protein   14.6g

Ingredients

1 lb extra-wide egg noodles
1 boxes instant mashed potatoes
1 large sweet onion, chopped
1 C. butter, melted
1 package Velveeta cheese, cubed
8 oz. cheddar cheese, shredded

8 oz. sauerkraut
1/4 C. butter, melted

Directions

1. Before you do anything, preheat the oven to 350 F.
2. Prepare the noodles by following the instructions on the package.
3. Prepare the mashed potatoes by following the instructions on the package.
4. Place a large pan over medium heat: Heat in it 1 C. of butter. Cook in it the onion with a pinch of salt for 6 min.
5. Get a large mixing bowl: Combine in it the mashed potato with onion, cheese, sauerkraut, a pinch of salt and pepper.
6. Spoon the mix into the greased casserole. Pour all over it 1/4 C. of melted butter. Place it in the oven and cook it for 46 min.
7. Serve it hot.
8. Enjoy.

BACK-TO-SCHOOL
Pierogies

Prep Time: 5 mins
Total Time: 30 mins

Servings per Recipe: 3
Calories   1071.9
Fat   91.8g
Cholesterol   258.4mg
Sodium   1463.8mg
Carbohydrates   5.4g
Protein   56.7g

Ingredients
24 oz. frozen pierogies
water
2 tbsp butter
2 tbsp olive oil
1/2 large onion, sliced thick
salt and pepper, to taste

Directions
1. Prepare the pierogies by following the instructions on the package.
2. Place a large pan over medium heat: Heat in it the butter with olive oil.
3. Cook in it the onion with pierogies, a pinch of salt and pepper for 5 to 7 min over high heat.
4. Serve them hot.
5. Enjoy.

Maine
Pierogies Plates

Prep Time: 5 mins
Total Time: 15 mins

Servings per Recipe: 6
Calories   82.1
Fat   3.5g
Cholesterol   7.6mg
Sodium   39.3mg
Carbohydrates   12.6g
Protein   2.3g

Ingredients

1 tsp Old Bay Seasoning
1/2 head green cabbage, quartered
2 ears corn, sliced 6 ways
8 oz. turkey kielbasa, sliced
1 1/2 tbsp butter, divided
1 boxes frozen potato pierogies

fresh parsley, chopped as garnish

Directions

1. Place a large pot over medium heat. Stir in it 1 C. of water with old bay seasoning. Bring them to a boil.
2. Stir in the cabbage, corn, kielbasa and 1/2 tbsp butter.
3. Put on the lid and let them cook for 10 to 12 min while stirring them every few minutes.
4. Place the pierogies on top then drizzle 1 tbsp of melted butter over them.
5. Stir them well then serve them warm.
6. Enjoy.

HERBED
Mushroom Pierogies

🥣 Prep Time: 15 mins
🕐 Total Time: 40 mins

Servings per Recipe: 4
Calories   386.2
Fat   34.9g
Cholesterol   38.3mg
Sodium   350.0mg
Carbohydrates   13.2g
Protein   7.9g

Ingredients

24 frozen potato cheese pierogi, thawed
4 tbsp olive oil
2 tbsp butter
6 slices bacon, chopped
1 large onion, sliced
4 garlic cloves, chopped
8 oz. sliced mushrooms

1 lb cabbage, thinly sliced
1/4 C. water
salt and pepper
1/3 C. fresh dill, chopped
sour cream, for serving

Directions

1. Place a large pan over medium heat: Melt in it 1 tbsp of butter and oil.
2. Cook in it the pierogies for 5 to 6 min on each side until they become golden brown while adding more butter if needed.
3. Drain the pierogies and place them aside.
4. Heat 1 tbsp of oil in the same pan. Cook in it the bacon until it becomes crisp. Drain it and place it aside.
5. Discard 2/3 of the fat in the pan. Heat 1 tbsp of oil in the same pan.
6. Cook in it the onions, mushrooms and garlic for 9 min.
7. Stir in the cabbage, water, salt, pepper. Put on the lid and let them cook for 3 to 4 min.
8. Place the pierogies on serving plates then top them with the cabbage and bacon. Serve them warm.
9. Enjoy.

Diane's
Potluck Pierogies

🥣 Prep Time: 30 mins
🕐 Total Time: 55 mins

Servings per Recipe: 6
Calories	718.4
Fat	28.7g
Cholesterol	39.5mg
Sodium	818.5mg
Carbohydrates	93.7g
Protein	22.5g

Ingredients

3 lbs potatoes, chunked, boiled
2 C. shredded sharp cheddar cheese
1 tsp salt
1/2 tsp pepper
1/2 C. margarine
4 C. sliced onions

1 packages jumbo pasta shells, cooked

Directions

1. Before you do anything, preheat the oven to 350 F. Grease a casserole dish with some butter.
2. Get a large mixing bowl: Mix in it the potato with cheese, a pinch of salt and pepper until they become smooth.
3. Place a large pan over medium heat: Het in it the margarine. Cook in it the onion for 12 to 16 min.
4. Lay half of the onion in the casserole.
5. Spoon the potato mix into the pasta shells and place them over the onion layer. Top it with the remaining onion.
6. Place the casserole in the oven and let it cool for 24 to 26 min. Serve it hot.
7. Enjoy.

SPICY
Sausage Pierogies

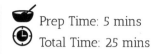

Prep Time: 5 mins
Total Time: 25 mins

Servings per Recipe: 4
Calories   259.6
Fat   22.5g
Cholesterol   51.8mg
Sodium   498.5mg
Carbohydrates   2.8g
Protein   10.6g

Ingredients
1 lb pierogi, frozen
3 slices turkey bacon
1 onion, chopped
4 beef sausages, spicy
sour cream

Directions
1. Bring a large salted pot of water to a boil. Cook in it the pierogies for 10 to 14 min.
2. Remove the pierogies from the water and place them aside to drain.
3. Place a large pan over medium heat: Cook in it the bacon until it becomes crisp. Drain it and place it aside.
4. Add the sausages to the same pan and cook them for 12 to 14 min. Drain them and place them aside.
5. Add the pierogies to the same pan and cook them for 8 to 10 min until they become golden brown.
6. Stir in the cooked bacon with onion and sausages. Serve your pierogies hot with some sour cream.
7. Enjoy.

White Cheese
Pierogies with Peas

Prep Time: 5 mins
Total Time: 15 mins

Servings per Recipe: 4
Calories	133.4
Fat	4.9g
Cholesterol	32.8mg
Sodium	893.2mg
Carbohydrates	5.5g
Protein	16.0g

Ingredients

1 package frozen pierogi, potato and onion
or potato and cheese
1 jars alfredo sauce
1 1/2 C. diced ham, optional
1 C. frozen baby peas
black pepper

1/4 C. grated parmesan cheese

Directions

1. Bring a large salted pot of water to a boil. Cook in it the pierogies for 4 to 5 min. Drain them and place them aside.
2. Place a large pan over medium heat: Stir in it the ham with peas, alfredo sauce, a pinch of salt and pepper.
3. Let the cook for 10 to 12 min over low heat. Spoon the sauce over the pierogies then serve them hot.
4. Enjoy.

PIEROGI
Lasagna I

🥣 Prep Time: 15 mins
🕐 Total Time: 45 mins

Servings per Recipe: 4

Calories	1087.2
Fat	69.1g
Cholesterol	289.1mg
Sodium	1034.9mg
Carbohydrates	85.9g
Protein	31.1g

Ingredients

15 lasagna noodles
2 eggs
2 C. cheddar cheese, grated
2 C. mashed potatoes
pepper, to taste
garlic salt, to taste
onion powder, to taste

1 C. butter
1 onion, chopped
sour cream

Directions

1. Before you do anything, preheat the oven to 350 F. Grease a casserole dish with some butter.
2. Prepare the lasagna noodles by following the instructions on the package.
3. Get a large mixing bowl: Combine in it the potatoes, cheese, egg, and spices.
4. Place 1/3 of the noodles in the casserole then top it with half of the potato mix.
5. Lay another 1/3 of noodles on top followed by the remaining potato mix and noodles at the end.
6. Place a large skillet over medium heat. Heat in it the butter. Sauté in it the onion with a pinch of salt for 6 to 8 min.
7. Spread the onion over the noodles layer then cover the casserole with a piece of foil.
8. Bake the lasagna for 32 min. allow it to sit for 5 min then serve it warm.
9. Enjoy.

Creamy
Pot Stickers

Prep Time: 1 mins
Total Time: 15 mins

Servings per Recipe: 4
Calories   188.5
Fat   20.0g
Cholesterol   52.8mg
Sodium   125.0mg
Carbohydrates   1.8g
Protein   1.3g

Ingredients

3 tbsp butter, softened
1 lb frozen potato pierogi
1 C. water
salt and pepper
2 tbsp dill, chopped
2 tbsp chives, chopped

2 tbsp flat-leaf parsley, chopped
1 C. sour cream

Directions

1. Place a large skillet over medium heat. Coat it with butter.
2. Place in it the pierogies then pour over them 1 C. of water. Put on the lid and let them cook for 9 min over high heat.
3. Once the time is up, remove the cover. Allow the pierogies to cook until the water evaporates and they stick slightly to the pan and become crisp on the bottom.
4. Remove the pierogies from the pan and place them on a serving plate.
5. Stir the sour cream with herbs, a pinch of salt and pepper in the pan. Heat it for 1 to 2 min then pour it over the pierogies and serve them warm.
6. Enjoy.

6-INGREDIENT
Pierogies I

🥣 Prep Time: 1 hr
🕐 Total Time: 1 hr 30 mins

Servings per Recipe: 6
Calories   514.2
Fat   17.0g
Cholesterol   137.8mg
Sodium   106.5mg
Carbohydrates   76.1g
Protein   13.9g

Ingredients
3 C. flour
3 eggs, beaten
1 C. sour cream
4 medium potatoes, cooked and peeled
1 medium onion, diced
3 tbsp butter

Directions
1. Place a large pan over medium heat: Heat in it the butter. Add the onion with a pinch of salt and cook it for 4 min.
2. Get a large mixing bowl: Mix in the potato with onion, a pinch of salt and pepper until they become smooth to make the filling.
3. Get a large mixing bowl: Mix in it the flour with eggs, sour cream, and a pinch of salt.
4. Shape the dough into a ball and cover it with a paper towel. Place it aside to rest for 35 min.
5. Once the time is up, place the dough on floured surface. Flatten dough with a rolling pin until it become 1/4 inch thick.
6. Use a 3 inches cookie cutter to cut the dough into circles. Place about 1 full tbsp of the filling on the side of 1 dough circle.
7. Pull the other half of the circle over the filling. Wet the edges of the circle with some water then press it with a fork to seal the edges.
8. Bring a large salted pot of water to a boil. Cook in it the pierogies in batches for 3 to 4 min until they rise on top.
9. Drain the pierogies then serve them with your favorite toppings.
10. Enjoy.

Pier-A
Pierogies

🥣 Prep Time: 15 mins
🕐 Total Time: 50 mins

Servings per Recipe: 4
Calories   141.3
Fat   9.9g
Cholesterol   9.5mg
Sodium   543.7mg
Carbohydrates   9.7g
Protein   3.9g

Ingredients

1 packages potato & cheese pierogies
1 tbsp margarine
1 medium onion, diced
1 green pepper, diced
1 cans cream of mushroom soup
1/4 C. milk

1/4 C. cheddar cheese, shredded

Directions

1. Before you do anything, preheat the oven to 350 F. Grease a baking dish with some butter.
2. Bring a large salted pot of water to a boil. Cook in it the pierogies for 6 to 8 min. Remove them from the water and place them aside.
3. Place a small pan over medium heat: Melt in it the margarine. Cook in it the green pepper with onion for 6 min.
4. Lay the pierogies in the baking dish then top it with onion mix.
5. Get a large mixing bowl: Whisk in it the mushroom soup with milk, a pinch of salt and pepper.
6. Pour the mix all over the pierogies then sprinkle the cheese all over them.
7. Place the dish in the oven and let it cook for 37 min. Serve it hot.
8. Enjoy.

BACKROAD SQUASH
Pierogies Stir Fry

Prep Time: 15 mins
Total Time: 35 mins

Servings per Recipe: 2
Calories   443.6
Fat   28.5g
Cholesterol   22.0mg
Sodium   1075.0mg
Carbohydrates   34.4g
Protein   18.6g

Ingredients
1 box pierogies
3 tbsp olive oil
2 medium onions, sliced
1 1/2 C. carrots, sliced
1 lb asparagus, sliced
1 medium sized yellow squash, sliced
1 tbsp chopped garlic

1/2 tsp salt
1/4 tsp ground black pepper
1/2 C. parmesan cheese, grated

Directions
1. Prepare the pierogies by following the instructions on the package.
2. Place a large pan over medium heat: Heat the oil in it. Cook in it the carrot with onion and a pinch of salt for 5 min.
3. Stir in the squash with asparagus then cook them for 6 min.
4. Mix in the garlic with a pinch of salt and pepper. Cook them for 3 min while stirring them often.
5. Add the pierogies to the pan and toss them gently with the veggies. Serve them hot with parmesan cheese on top.
6. Get a large mixing bowl:
7. Enjoy.

Tarragon Pierogies

🥣 Prep Time: 45 mins

🕐 Total Time: 1 hr 25 mins

Servings per Recipe: 1

Calories	82.2
Fat	3.2g
Cholesterol	0.0mg
Sodium	171.4mg
Carbohydrates	11.6g
Protein	2.1g

Ingredients

1 C. white flour
1 C. wheat flour
3/4 C. warm water
1/4 C. oil
1 tsp salt
1 medium onion, finely diced
2 celery ribs, finely diced
1 carrot, grated
3 small red potatoes, finely diced
3 garlic cloves, minced

1 cans peas, drained
1 tsp salt
1 tsp ground black pepper
1 tsp sage
1 - 2 tsp thyme
1 - 2 tsp tarragon
1 tbsp oil
2 - 3 tbsp margarine

Directions

1. To prepare the dough:
2. Get a large mixing bowl: Mix in it the flour with water, oil, and salt. Shape the dough into a bowl and wrap it in a piece of plastic.
3. Let the dough rest for 32 min.
4. Place a large pan over medium heat: Heat the oil in it. Cook in it the garlic for 1 min. Stir in the onion and cook them for 3 min.
5. Stir in the carrots, celery, potatoes and seasonings. Cook them for 8 to 10 min over low medium heat while stirring them often.
6. When the veggies are done, place the pan aside to cool down.
7. Place the dough on a floured surface and flatten it then use a cookie cutter to cut it into circles.
8. Divide the filling between the dough circles and place it on one side of each dough circle.
9. Pull the other half of the dough over the filling and press it with a fork to seal it.
10. Place a large salted pot of water to a boil. Cook it until it starts boiling.
11. Place in it the pierogies and cook them for 4 to 6 min until they rise on top. Drain the pierogies then serve them with your favorite toppings.
12. Enjoy.

POLISH
Pierogies I

Prep Time: 2 hr 30 mins
Total Time: 2 hr 40 mins

Servings per Recipe: 1
Calories	49.8
Fat	2.5g
Cholesterol	30.0mg
Sodium	67.9mg
Carbohydrates	4.3g
Protein	2.3g

Ingredients
4 large eggs, separated
2 lbs fresh cheese
1/2 C. all-purpose flour
salt
2 oz. butter
1/2 C. plain breadcrumbs
sour cream, for serving

sugar, for serving

Directions
1. To make the dough; Beat the egg whites until they become like foam.
2. Get a large mixing bowl: Mix it the flour with cheese, egg yolks and a pinch of salt. Fold the mix into the egg whites.
3. Shape the dough into a ball then wrap it in a piece of plastic. Place it in the fridge to rest for 2 h.
4. Place 1 large tbsp of dough on a floured surface. Roll it in the shape of a log then slice it into pieces and flatten them a bit.
5. Repeat the process with the remaining dough.
6. Place a large pot of salted water over medium heat. Drop in it the pierogies and cook them until they float on top.
7. Place a large pan over medium heat. Heat in it the butter until it melts. Cook in it the breadcrumbs until they become golden.
8. Serve your pierogies with the golden crumbs and sour cream.
9. Enjoy.

Pierogi
Lunch Box

Prep Time: 5 mins
Total Time: 25 mins

Servings per Recipe: 1
Calories   483.5
Fat   54.2g
Cholesterol   0.0mg
Sodium   1491.7mg
Carbohydrates   0.9g
Protein   0.2g

Ingredients

1/4 C. olive oil
4 tbsp Frank's red hot sauce
1 tbsp Lawry's Seasoned Salt
1 boxes frozen pierogies

Directions

1. Before you do anything, preheat the oven to 400 F. Coat a baking sheet with some butter or a cooking spray.
2. Get a large mixing bowl: Combine in it the hot sauce with oil and salt.
3. Lay the pierogies on the greased baking sheet. Drizzle the sauce mix all over them.
4. Place the pan in the oven and let it cook for 22 min. Serve right away.
5. Enjoy.

30-MINUTE
Polish Pierogies

Prep Time: 10 mins
Total Time: 30 mins

Servings per Recipe: 4
Calories	461.0
Fat	41.3g
Cholesterol	74.7mg
Sodium	1110.9mg
Carbohydrates	7.1g
Protein	14.5g

Ingredients
3 tbsp olive oil, divided
1 large yellow onion, thinly sliced
1 lb frozen potato and cheddar pierogies
1 lb turkey kielbasa, sliced
2 tbsp apple cider vinegar
2 tbsp whole grain mustard
fresh parsley, chopped

Directions
1. Place a heavy saucepan over medium heat. Heat 2 tbsp of olive oil. Cook in it the onion for 16 to 22 min.
2. Spread the onion in the pan. Place over it the pierogies and put on the lid then let it cook for 6 min.
3. Stir in the sausage pieces and cook them for 4 to 6 min while stirring them often.
4. Get a small mixing bowl: Whisk in it the vinegar, mustard and remaining olive oil to make the sauce.
5. Stir the sauce into the pierogies pan with a pinch of salt and pepper. Serve it hot.
6. Enjoy.

Breaded Pierogies

Prep Time: 5 mins
Total Time: 25 mins

Servings per Recipe: 1
Calories	389.4
Fat	31.0g
Cholesterol	86.6mg
Sodium	753.9mg
Carbohydrates	13.9g
Protein	14.4g

Ingredients

10 -12 potato & cheese pierogies
1 onion, diced
olive oil
cooking spray
6 tbsp butter
salt

1/2 C. seasoned bread crumbs
1 C. cheddar cheese, shredded
1/2 C. parmesan cheese

Directions

1. Before you do anything, preheat the oven to 350 F. Grease a casserole dish with some butter.
2. Bring a large salted pot of water to a boil. Place in it the pierogies and coo them for 4 to 5 min.
3. Place a large pan over medium heat: Drain the pierogies and cook them with 2 tbsp of butter, a pinch of salt and pepper for 1 to 2 min.
4. Spoon the pierogies into the casserole. Top it with the onion, parmesan cheese, cheddar cheese and bread crumbs.
5. Dot it with 4 tbsp of butter. Cover the pan with a piece of oil. Place it in the oven and let it cool for 16 min.
6. Once the time is up, discard the piece of foil. Bake it for an extra 12 to 16 min. Serve it hot.
7. Enjoy.

DOWNSTATE
Pierogies

Prep Time: 10 mins
Total Time: 20 mins

Servings per Recipe: 32
Calories 69.3
Fat 1.0g
Cholesterol 0.0mg
Sodium 82.5mg
Carbohydrates 12.1g
Protein 2.7g

Ingredients
4 C. flour
1 tsp salt
2 tsp vegetable oil
1/4 tsp baking powder
1 1/4 C. warm water
16 oz. firm tofu, drained, pressed, crumbled
sugar

1 pinch salt
oil

Directions
1. Get a large mixing bowl: Mix in it the flour with oil, water, baking powder, oil and salt until you get a soft dough.
2. Place the dough on a floured surface and knead it for 6 min. Wrap it in a piece of plastic then place it in the fridge and let it rest for 2 h.
3. Get a mixing bowl: Toss in it the tofu with a pinch of salt and sugar.
4. Place the dough on a floured surface and flatten it until it becomes 1/8 inch thick.
5. Use 4 inches cookie cutter to cut it into circles. Place 1 tbsp of the filling on the side of each dough circle.
6. Pull the other side of the dough over the filling and press it with a fork to seal it.
7. Bring a large salted pot of water to a boil. Cook in it the pierogies for 6 to 7 min until they rise on top.
8. Drain the pierogies and serve them.
9. Enjoy.

Upstate
Pierogies

Prep Time: 5 mins
Total Time: 25 mins

Servings per Recipe: 4
Calories	32.7
Fat	3.5g
Cholesterol	0.0mg
Sodium	465.9mg
Carbohydrates	0.4g
Protein	0.1g

Ingredients
5 tbsp hot pepper sauce
1 tbsp oil
1/2 tsp cayenne pepper
1 package frozen pierogi

Directions
1. Before you do anything, preheat the oven to 400 F. Grease a cookie sheet with some butter.
2. Get a large mixing bowl: Whisk in it the hot sauce with oil and cayenne pepper. Stir the pierogies into the sauce.
3. Place the saucy pierogies on the cookie sheet. Bake them for 10 min. Flip them and cook them for an extra 10 min.
4. Serve them hot with your favorite sauce.
5. Enjoy.

PIEROGI
Milanese

🍳 Prep Time: 5 mins
🕐 Total Time: 5 hr 5 mins

Servings per Recipe: 5
Calories	73.4
Fat	3.0g
Cholesterol	0.0mg
Sodium	341.6mg
Carbohydrates	11.9g
Protein	1.6g

Ingredients

1 cans crushed tomatoes
1 shallot, sliced
1 C. chopped green bell pepper
1 tbsp olive oil
1/2 tbsp red wine vinegar
1/2-1 tsp dried Italian seasoning
black pepper

1 lb potato-filled pierogi, fresh or frozen

Directions

1. Stir the crushed tomatoes, shallots, peppers, oil, vinegar, Italian seasoning and black pepper in a slow cooker.
2. Put on the lid and cook them for 7 h on low or 4 on high.
3. Stir in the pierogies and put on the lid. Cook them for 1 h on low. Serve them warm.
4. Enjoy.

Velveeta
Lasagna

🥣 Prep Time: 15 mins

🕐 Total Time: 1 hr 15 mins

Servings per Recipe: 1
Calories	5978.1
Fat	334.0g
Cholesterol	968.4mg
Sodium	8501.1mg
Carbohydrates	613.8g
Protein	149.2g

Ingredients

9 -12 lasagna noodles
1 1/4 C. butter
4 medium onions, sliced
10 -12 medium potatoes, peeled and cubed
1 dash salt and black pepper

1 (1 lb) box Velveeta cheese, cubed
grated parmesan cheese

Directions

1. Before you do anything, preheat the oven to 350 F. Grease a casserole dish with some butter.
2. Cook the lasagna noodles by following the instructions on the box.
3. Place a large pan over medium heat: Heat 1 stick of butter in it. Add the onion and cook it for 3 min.
4. Get a large mixing bowl: Press in it the potato until it become smooth.
5. Mix in the cheese, salt, pepper, and remaining butter.
6. Place 1/3 of the noodles in the casserole dish. Top it with 1/3 of the onion followed by 1/3 of the potato mixture.
7. Repeat the process to make more layers. Top the lasagna with cheese then cook it in the oven for 32 to 36 min. Serve it hot.
8. Enjoy.

HOMEMADE
Pierogies Dough

Prep Time: 10 mins
Total Time: 20 mins

Servings per Recipe: 1
Calories   79.4
Fat   2.5g
Cholesterol   9.3mg
Sodium   26.0mg
Carbohydrates   12.0g
Protein   1.9g

Ingredients
6 C. flour
1/2 C. margarine, diced
2 eggs
1/4 C. sour cream
1 1/4 C. potato water

Directions
1. Place a large pan over medium heat: Mix in it the flour with margarine and a pinch of salt until they become coarse.
2. Mix in the eggs, water and sour cream until you get a soft dough. Cover the dough completely with a plastic wrap.
3. Place the dough in the fridge to rest for 35 min.
4. Use the dough to make you pierogies with the filling that you desire.
5. Enjoy.

5-Ingredient
Pierogies

🥣 Prep Time: 30 mins
🕐 Total Time: 1 hr 15 mins

Servings per Recipe: 20
Calories   206.7
Fat   22.1g
Cholesterol   78.1mg
Sodium   43.8mg
Carbohydrates   1.9g
Protein   1.1g

Ingredients

2 1/4 lb pierogies
4 1/4 C. whipping cream
6 tbsp butter
1 medium onion, chopped
salt and pepper

Directions

1. Before you do anything, preheat the oven to 350 F. Coat a casserole dish with some butter.
2. Cook the pierogies according to the instructions on the package until they become dente.
3. Drain the pierogies and place half of them in the greased dish.
4. Top them with 3 tbsp of butter then repeat the process to make another layer.
5. Season them with some salt and pepper. Pour the whipping cream all over them. Cover it with a piece of foil.
6. Bake the pierogies casserole in the oven for 35 to 46 min. Serve it hot.
7. Enjoy.

TURKISH
Pierogies

Prep Time: 10 mins
Total Time: 20 mins

Servings per Recipe: 4
Calories	147.0
Fat	10.9g
Cholesterol	0.0mg
Sodium	25.9mg
Carbohydrates	11.3g
Protein	2.8g

Ingredients

2 medium onions, quartered lengthwise and sliced
3 tbsp vegetable oil
1 tsp caraway seed
1 Turkish bay leaves
15 oz. diced tomatoes
1 C. chicken broth

1 tsp sugar
1/4 C. chopped dill
24 frozen potato-cheddar pierogies
sour cream

Directions

1. Prepare the pierogies according to the instructions on the package.
2. Place a large pan over medium heat: Heat the oil in it. Sauté in it the caraway seeds and bay leaf for 40 sec.
3. Stir in the onion and cook them for 14 to 16 min. Turn up the heat and let it cook until it become caramelized.
4. Add the tomato with broth, sugar, 3/4 tsp salt, and 1/2 tsp pepper. Cook it for 4 min.
5. Discard the bay leaf then stir the dill into the sauce. Serve your pierogies hot with the sauce.
6. Enjoy.

Pennsylvania
Pierogies

Prep Time: 10 mins
Total Time: 25 mins

Servings per Recipe: 4
Calories	64.6
Fat	2.4g
Cholesterol	55.0mg
Sodium	121.5mg
Carbohydrates	6.6g
Protein	3.7g

Ingredients

1 egg, beaten
1/3 C. Italian style breadcrumbs
2 tbsp grated parmesan cheese
1 packages frozen potato & cheese
pierogies

Directions

1. Before you do anything, preheat the oven to 400 F. Grease a cookie sheet with some butter.
2. Place a large pan over medium heat: Whisk in it the egg with 1 tbsp of water.
3. Mix the cheese with breadcrumbs in a shallow bowl and place it aside.
4. Coat the pierogies with egg then roll it in the cheese mix. Place the pierogies on the cookie sheet then bake them for 16 min.
5. Serve your golden pierogies with your favorite sauce.
6. Enjoy.

VEGAN
Pierogies Dough

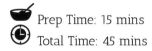

Prep Time: 15 mins
Total Time: 45 mins

Servings per Recipe: 1
Calories	61.5
Fat	1.9g
Cholesterol	0.0mg
Sodium	39.2mg
Carbohydrates	9.5g
Protein	1.2g

Ingredients
3 C. all-purpose flour
1/2 tsp salt
1/4 C. oil
1 C. water

Directions
1. Get a large mixing bowl: Mix in it the flour with oil, water and salt until you get a smooth dough.
2. Place the dough on a floured surface and knead it for 5 min. Cover the dough complete with a plastic wrap and place it aside to sit for 32 min.
3. Enjoy.

Seafood Pierogies

Prep Time: 45 mins
Total Time: 55 mins

Servings per Recipe: 1	
Calories	50.2
Fat	1.2g
Cholesterol	19.4mg
Sodium	35.7mg
Carbohydrates	7.7g
Protein	1.7g

Ingredients

2 large eggs
1/4 tsp salt
1/2 tsp Old Bay Seasoning
2 C. flour
2 oz. cream cheese
water

1 1/2 C. mashed potatoes
1 C. crab claw meat
1 tsp Old Bay Seasoning
lemon dill seasoning
butter
sautéed onion

Directions

1. To make the Dough:
2. Get a large mixing bowl: Mix in it the flour with cream cheese, eggs and salt then mix them well.
3. Shape the dough into a ball and wrap it in a plastic wrap. Place it aside to rest for 24 to 26 min.
4. To make the filling:
5. Get a mixing bowl: Mix in it the mashed potato with crab meat, old bay seasoning, lemon seasoning, a pinch of salt and pepper.
6. Flatten the dough on a floured surface until it becomes thin. Use a 4 inches cookie cutter to cut it into circles.
7. Place 1 to 2 tbsp of the filling on one side of a dough circle.
8. Pull the other side of the dough over the filling and press it with a fork to seal it.
9. Bring a large salted pot of water to a boil. Cook in it the pierogies for 6 to 7 min until they rise on top.
10. Drain the pierogies and sauté them with some butter and onion in a large skillet or serve them as they are with some melted butter.
11. Enjoy.

BACON
Pierogies

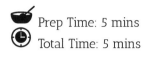
Prep Time: 5 mins
Total Time: 5 mins

Servings per Recipe: 9
Calories   243.3
Fat   5.8g
Cholesterol   28.9mg
Sodium   96.6mg
Carbohydrates   40.1g
Protein   6.5g

Ingredients

2 C. meat pieces
2 slices bread, wet, squeezed
1 onion, chopped
1 tbsp shortening
salt and pepper
3 slices turkey bacon, diced and cooked
1 egg

3 1/4 C. flour
salt
1/2 C. water
1 1/2 tbsp butter, melted
1 1/2 tbsp breadcrumbs

Directions

1. To make the filling:
2. Get a food processor: Pulse in it the meat with bread crumbs until they become lean.
3. Place a large pan over medium heat: Melt in it the shortening. Cook in it the onion for 4 min.
4. Add to it the meat mixture, a pinch of salt and pepper. Cook them for 8 min. Place it aside to cool down.
5. To make the dough:
6. Get a large mixing bowl: ix in it the flour wit egg and a pinch fo salt.
7. Place the dough on a floured surface and knead it until the dough becomes soft.
8. Flatten the dough until it becomes slightly thin. Cut it into 3 inches squares.
9. Divide the filling between the dough squares by placing them on the side.
10. Fold the dough over the filling in the shape of triangle and press the edges to seal them.
11. Bring a large salted pot of water to a boil. Cook in it the pierogies for 6 to 7 min until they rise on top.
12. Place a large skillet over medium heat. Stir in it the butter with breadcrumbs.
13. Add the pierogies and cook them for 2 to 4 min then serve them hot.
14. Enjoy.

Pierogies Parm

🥣 Prep Time: 20 mins
🕐 Total Time: 50 mins

Servings per Recipe: 4
Calories	233.0
Fat	13.7g
Cholesterol	2.5mg
Sodium	529.9mg
Carbohydrates	24.9g
Protein	3.1g

Ingredients

1 packages frozen pierogies
2 C. marinara sauce
2 large onions, thinly sliced
1 packages mushrooms, thinly sliced
1/4 C. grated parmesan cheese
3 tbsp oil
1 garlic clove, minced
salt and pepper

Directions

1. Before you do anything, preheat the oven to 350 F. Grease a casserole dish with some butter.
2. Bring a large salted pot of water to a boil. Cook in it the pierogies for 3 to 5 min until they rise on top.
3. Place a large pan over medium heat. Heat the oil in it. Add the garlic with onion and mushroom. Cook them for 4 min.
4. Stir in the marinara sauce with a pinch of salt and pepper. Cook them until they start boiling. Let them cook for 6 min over low heat.
5. Place the pierogies in the greased dish. Pour the marinara sauce all over them.
6. Use piece of foil to cover the dish. Place it in the oven and let it cook for 32 min.
7. Discard the foil and top the pierogies casserole with some cheese then serve it hot.
8. Enjoy.

PORTUGUESE
Pierogies

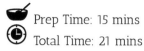 Prep Time: 15 mins

Total Time: 21 mins

Servings per Recipe: 4
Calories	292.8
Fat	22.0g
Cholesterol	49.9mg
Sodium	1019.9mg
Carbohydrates	8.5g
Protein	15.7g

Ingredients
4 C. water
12 7/8 oz. frozen potato and onion filled
pierogies
8 oz. uncooked chorizo sausage
1 pint red cherry tomatoes
8 oz. tomato sauce
4 oz. watercress

Directions
1. Bring a large salted pot of water to a boil. Cook in it the pierogies for 6 to 7 min until they rise on top.
2. Place a large pan over medium heat: Cook in it the chorizo for 8 min. discard the fat.
3. Stir in 3 1/2 C. of tomato sauce with tomato sauce then cook them for 7 to 9 min.
4. Place the pierogies in serving plates with the marinara sauce. Garnish them with the remaining cherry tomato.
5. Enjoy.

6-Ingredient
Pierogies

🥣 Prep Time: 15 mins
🕐 Total Time: 60 mins

Servings per Recipe: 4
Calories   246.7
Fat   10.9g
Cholesterol   65.0mg
Sodium   647.3mg
Carbohydrates   13.0g
Protein   23.4g

Ingredients

1 dozen frozen potato & cheese pierogi, thawed
1 cans cream of chicken soup
3/4 C. milk
1 cans sliced mushrooms, drained
1 C. frozen peas

2 C. cubed cooked chicken

Directions

1. Before you do anything, preheat the oven to 350 F.
2. Grease a baking dish with some butter. Lay in it the pierogies and place it aside.
3. Get a large mixing bowl: Whisk in it the soup, milk, mushrooms, peas, chicken, a pinch of salt and pepper.
4. Pour the mixture all over the pierogies. Place the casserole in the oven and let it cook for 48 min. Serve it hot.
5. Enjoy.

PICANTE
Pierogies

Prep Time: 5 mins
Total Time: 15 mins

Servings per Recipe: 4

Calories	286.4
Fat	15.6g
Cholesterol	47.7mg
Sodium	1120.1mg
Carbohydrates	25.6g
Protein	15.3g

Ingredients
1 package frozen potato and onion pierogi
1 cans chili with beans
1 C. salsa or 1 C. picante sauce
1 C. frozen corn
1 C. shredded sharp cheddar cheese

Directions
1. Bring a large salted pot of water to a boil. Cook in it the pierogies for 6 to 7 min until they rise on top.
2. Place a large pan over medium heat. Bring in it the picante sauce with chili beans to a boil.
3. Lower the heat and stir in it the corn. Let them cook for 7 min.
4. Stir the pierogies into the sauce then top them with cheese. Serve it hot.
5. Enjoy.

Green
Mozzarella Pierogies

🥣 Prep Time: 10 mins
🕐 Total Time: 35 mins

Servings per Recipe: 6
Calories   83.5
Fat   5.5g
Cholesterol   7.3mg
Sodium   445.4mg
Carbohydrates   4.8g
Protein   4.2g

Ingredients
1 dozen frozen potato and onion pierogies
1 cans cream of mushroom soup
5 oz. chopped fresh spinach
2 tbsp chopped onions
1 garlic clove, minced
1/2 tsp olive oil

1/4 C. mozzarella cheese
1/4 C. parmesan cheese

Directions
1. Before you do anything, preheat the oven to 350 F. Grease a casserole dish with some butter.
2. Bring a large salted pot of water to a boil. Cook in it the pierogies for 4 to 5 min until they rise on top.
3. Place a large pan over medium heat: Heat the oil in it. Sauté in it the onion with garlic for 4 min.
4. Add the spinach and cook them for 2 min. Stir in the soup and cook them for 4 min to make the sauce.
5. Spread 2 tbsp of the spinach sauce in the casserole dish. Top it with half of the pierogies then cover them with half of the sauce.
6. Repeat the process to make another layer. Sprinkle the parmesan and mozzarella cheese on top.
7. Place the casserole in the oven and let it cook for 22 min. serve it hot.
8. Enjoy.

SESAME
Pierogies with Chili Sauce

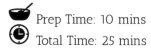 Prep Time: 10 mins

Total Time: 25 mins

Servings per Recipe: 4	
Calories	129.1
Fat	9.1g
Cholesterol	0.0mg
Sodium	1373.2mg
Carbohydrates	8.0g
Protein	5.7g

Ingredients
8 green onions, divided
1 1/2 C. chicken broth
1/2 C. water
2 tbsp peanut oil
4 slices fresh ginger, sliced thin
10 potato & cheese pierogies
1/4 C. cilantro leaves, chopped

1 tbsp toasted sesame seeds
1/3 C. soy sauce
1/4 C. orange juice
4 tsp rice wine vinegar
1 1/2 tsp crystallized ginger, minced
1 tbsp Asian hot chili oil
2 tsp minced garlic

Directions
1. Get a small mixing bowl: Whisk in it the soy sauce, orange juice, rice wine vinegar, crystallized ginger, hot chili oil and minced garlic to make the chili sauce.
2. Place a large pan over medium heat: Stir in it the broth, 1/2 C. water, peanut oil or canola oil or butter, and ginger.
3. Cook them until they start boiling. Lay the pierogies on top then lower the heat.
4. Sprinkle the green onion on top. Let the pierogies cook for 10 to 12 min. Discard the ginger.
5. Let them cook for 4 to 6 min or until the pierogies stick to the pan.
6. Garnish the pierogies with parsley and sesame seeds then serve them with the chili sauce.
7. Enjoy.

Italian
Curry Pierogies

🥣 Prep Time: 15 mins
🕐 Total Time: 55 mins

Servings per Recipe: 4
Calories	601.1
Fat	45.6g
Cholesterol	87.5mg
Sodium	1731.7mg
Carbohydrates	22.4g
Protein	26.3g

Ingredients
1 -1 1/4 lb turkey Italian sausage, links
3 tbsp butter
1 1/2 tbsp salad oil
2 medium white onions, sliced
1 red bell pepper, sliced
1/2 tsp kosher salt

1 tsp seasoned pepper
1 package pierogi, frozen
1/2 tsp garlic powder
2 tbsp Hungarian paprika
1 1/2-2 tsp curry powder
1/2 lb frozen peas

Directions
1. Place a large pan over medium heat: Cook in it the sausages with 1/4 C. of water for 6 min with the lid on.
2. Remove the lid and cook them sausage for an extra 14 min while flipping them often.
3. Place a large skillet over medium heat. Melt the butter with oil in it. Sauté in it the onion with bell pepper, a pinch of salt and pepper for 12 min.
4. Stir in the pierogies with garlic powder, paprika, curry powder, a pinch of salt and pepper. Cook them for 9 min while stirring them often.
5. Drain the sausages and slice them then stir them into the pierogies skillet along with the peas.
6. Cook them for 6 min. Lower the heat and put on the lid then let them cook for an extra 5 min. Serve them hot.
7. Enjoy.

GRANNY'S
Apple Pierogies

Prep Time: 15 mins
Total Time: 45 mins

Servings per Recipe: 4
Calories	112.4
Fat	6.9g
Cholesterol	0.0mg
Sodium	20.7mg
Carbohydrates	13.0g
Protein	1.4g

Ingredients
2 tbsp olive oil
1 medium onion, thin slices
10 oz. shredded red cabbage
1 garlic clove, minced
1 C. apple cider
1 pinch red pepper flakes
1 granny smith apple, chunks

16 oz. frozen potato and onion pierogies

Directions
1. Place a large pan over medium heat: Heat in it 1 tbsp oil.
2. Sauté in it the garlic with onion for 6 min. Stir in the cabbage, cider, 1/4 tsp salt, 1/4 tsp black pepper and a pinch of red pepper flakes.
3. Cook them over high heat for 3 min while stirring them often.
4. Add the apple chunks and cook them for 6 min.
5. Place a large pan over medium heat: Stir in it 1/2 C. of water and 1 tbsp of oil. Bring them to a simmer.
6. Stir in the pierogies then put on the lid and let them cook for 6 min.
7. Once the time is up, remove the lid and cook them for an extra 11 to 14 min. Stir in the cabbage mixture then season them with a pinch of salt and pepper.
8. Serve them hot.
9. Enjoy.

Bell Pierogies
with Tomato Sauce

🥣 Prep Time: 10 mins

🕐 Total Time: 28 mins

Servings per Recipe: 3

Calories	61.1
Fat	0.7g
Cholesterol	0.0mg
Sodium	795.7mg
Carbohydrates	13.4g
Protein	2.9g

Ingredients
1 bag frozen mixed peppers, stir-fry
1 packages potato & cheese pierogies
1 cans tomato sauce
1 tbsp finely chopped fresh oregano
2 tsp fennel seeds, ground
1/2 tsp salt

1/2 tsp ground black pepper

Directions
1. Place a large salted pot of water over high heat. Cook in it the pierogies for 4 to 6 min.
2. Place a large pan over medium heat: Grease it with a cooking spray.
3. Sauté in it the peppers with for 9 to 11 min. Stir in it the pierogies with 1/4 C. of its cooking liquid, tomato sauce, oregano, fennel, salt, and pepper to the pepper.
4. Cook them for 2 min. Serve your pierogies hot.
5. Enjoy.

MUSHROOM PIEROGIES
with Dill Cream Sauce

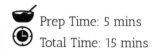 Prep Time: 5 mins

Total Time: 15 mins

Servings per Recipe: 6
Calories	79.2
Fat	6.6g
Cholesterol	17.9mg
Sodium	53.1mg
Carbohydrates	5.0g
Protein	2.2g

Ingredients
1 kg frozen pierogi
3 tbsp butter
1/2 red onion, sliced
8 oz. mushrooms, sliced
1 lemon
1/2 C. plain yogurt
2 tbsp fresh dill, chopped

Directions
1. Cook the pierogies by following the instructions on the package.
2. Place a large pan over medium heat: Heat in it the butter. Sauté in it the onion for 6 min.
3. Stir in the mushroom with a pinch of salt and cook them for another 6 min. Turn off the heat.
4. Get a small mixing bowl: Stir in it 2 tbsp of lemon juice, dill and yogurt to make the sauce.
5. Stir the sauce with pierogies into the mushroom pan. Cook them for 3 min while stirring them often then serve them.
6. Enjoy.

Pittsburgh
Pierogies

🥄 Prep Time: 2 hr
🕐 Total Time: 2 hr 10 mins

Servings per Recipe: 4
Calories   507.6
Fat   15.9g
Cholesterol   66.7mg
Sodium   773.1mg
Carbohydrates   64.0g
Protein   24.8g

Ingredients
2 1/2 C. flour, sifted
1 tsp salt
1 C. milk
1/4 C. margarine
3/4 C. dry curd cottage cheese
1 egg

salt
pepper
dill

Directions
1. Get a large mixing bowl: Mix in it the cottage cheese with egg, a pinch of salt and pepper to make the filling.
2. Place a heavy saucepan over medium heat. Heat in it the milk with margarine and bring them to a simmer.
3. Mix in the flour with a pinch of salt and whisk them until you get a smooth dough.
4. Place the dough on a floured surface and knead it until it becomes soft for several minutes.
5. Cut the dough in half then roll it into 1 inch log and slice into 3/4 pieces.
6. Press the dough slices slightly to flatten them. Place some of the filling in the middle then pull the dough edges on top and press them to seal them.
7. Repeat the process with the remaining dough and filling then place the pierogies on a lined up baking sheet.
8. Bring a large salted pot of water to a boil. Cook in it the pierogies in batches until they rise on top. Drain them then serve them with your favorite sauce.
9. Enjoy.

SWEET AND SOUR
Pierogies

Prep Time: 5 mins
Total Time: 5 mins

Servings per Recipe: 8
Calories	175.7
Fat	14.1g
Cholesterol	4.0mg
Sodium	671.2mg
Carbohydrates	11.7g
Protein	1.4g

Ingredients
2 dozen potato & cheese pierogies
3 tbsp vegetable oil
2 tsp Cajun seasoning
1/2 C. ketchup
1/2 C. hot mustard
1/2 C. BBQ sauce
1/2 C. ranch dressing

1/2 C. sweet and sour sauce

Directions
1. Fry the pierogies by following the instructions on the package.
2. Drain the pierogies and slice them in half then place them on serving plates. Season them with the Cajun seasoning.
3. Serve your pierogies along with the ketchup, mustard, barbecue sauce, ranch dressing and sour sauce.
4. Enjoy.

Wild Jerk
Pierogies

Prep Time: 40 mins
Total Time: 40 mins

Servings per Recipe: 4
Calories   213.0
Fat   4.5g
Cholesterol   0.0mg
Sodium   369.1mg
Carbohydrates   33.6g
Protein   10.5g

Ingredients

1 tbsp olive oil
1 1/4 C. green bell peppers, chopped
3/4 C. onion, chopped
1 1/2 C. sweet potatoes, cubed
1 cans chicken broth
1 tsp Jamaican jerk spice

1 boxes frozen potato and onion pierogies
1 cans black beans, drained and rinsed

Directions

1. Place a pot over medium heat. Heat the oil in it. Sauté in it the onion with pepper and a pinch of salt for 4 min.
2. Add the sweet potato cubes, broth and home-spice blend or jerk seasoning. Cook them until they start boiling.
3. Lower the heat and let them cook for 16 min while stirring them every once in a while. Stir in the beans and cook them for 3 min.
4. Mash the sauce mix slightly with a fork.
5. Prepare the pierogies by following the instructions on the package.
6. Drain them and serve them with the bean sauce.
7. Enjoy.

GERMAN HOMEMADE
Cheddar Pierogies

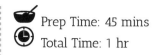
Prep Time: 45 mins
Total Time: 1 hr

Servings per Recipe: 4
Calories   1001.6
Fat   38.2g
Cholesterol   151.5mg
Sodium   815.8mg
Carbohydrates   133.4g
Protein   32.6g

Ingredients
2 C. flour
1/2 tsp salt
1 large egg
1/2 C. sour cream
1/4 C. butter, small pieces
5 large potatoes, cooked and mashed
1 large onion, chopped

8 oz. grated cheddar cheese

Directions
1. To make the dough:
2. Get a large mixing bowl: Mix in it the flour with salt. Add the egg with 1/2 C. of sour cream and butter. Mix them well until you get a soft dough.
3. Cover the dough with a piece of plastic wrap. Place it in the fridge for 28 to 32 min.
4. To make the filling:
5. Place a small skillet over medium heat. Melt in it some butter. Cook in it the onion for 5 min.
6. Get a large mixing bowl: Mix in it the onion with potato, cheese, a pinch of salt and pepper.
7. Place the dough on a floured surface then roll it until it becomes thin.
8. Use a 3 inches cookie cutter to cut the dough into circles.
9. Divide the filling between the dough circles on one side. Pull the other side over the filling and press the edges with a fork to seal them.
10. Bring a large salted pot of water to a boil. Lower in it the pierogies and cook them for 5 to 6 min until they rise on top.
11. Drain the pierogies and serve them with your favorite sauce.
12. Enjoy.

Jumbo
Pierogies Shells

Prep Time: 15 mins
Total Time: 45 mins

Servings per Recipe: 8
Calories	212.4
Fat	10.0g
Cholesterol	31.9mg
Sodium	521.3mg
Carbohydrates	21.3g
Protein	9.3g

Ingredients

25 uncooked jumbo pasta shells
1 packages refrigerated mashed potatoes
1 tbsp dried onion flakes
1/4 tsp onion powder
1/4 tsp garlic powder
2 C. shredded cheddar cheese, divided

1/4 C. green onion, chopped

Directions

1. Before you do anything, preheat the oven to 350 F. Grease a casserole dish with some butter.
2. Prepare pasta shells by following the instructions on the package.
3. Get a microwave safe bowl: Place in it the potato and cook it in the microwave for 3 min.
4. Get a large mixing bowl: Mix in it the mashed potato with minced onion, onion powder and garlic powder, 1 C. of cheese, a pinch of salt and pepper.
5. Spoon the filling into the pasta shells then place them in the greased casserole. Sprinkle the remaining cheese on top.
6. Place a piece of foil over the casserole to cover it. Cook it in the oven for 22 min.
7. Discard the foil and cook it for an extra 12 min. Serve it warm.
8. Enjoy.

FRENCH
Pierogies with Gravy

Prep Time: 20 mins
Total Time: 1 hr 15 mins

Servings per Recipe: 6

Calories	256.7
Fat	10.0g
Cholesterol	75.0mg
Sodium	660.6mg
Carbohydrates	13.4g
Protein	28.1g

Ingredients
1 1/2 lbs boneless skinless chicken breasts,
chunks
2 cans gravy
1 packages frozen potato pierogi, thawed
1 packages frozen mixed vegetables
salt and pepper
1 cans French-fried onions

Directions
1. Before you do anything, preheat the oven to 350 F. Grease a casserole dish with a cooking spray or butter.
2. Get a large mixing bowl: Mix in it the chicken, chicken gravy, pierogies, frozen vegetables, a pinch of salt and pepper.
3. Pour the mix into the greased casserole. Place a piece of foil over it to cover it then bake it for 52 min.
4. Once the time is up, discard the foil and bake the casserole for an extra 6 min. Serve it hot.
5. Enjoy.

Grilled
Parmesan Pierogies

🥣 Prep Time: 10 mins
🕐 Total Time: 20 mins

Servings per Recipe: 1
Calories   107.0
Fat   2.4g
Cholesterol   28.0mg
Sodium   24.2mg
Carbohydrates   17.7g
Protein   3.4g

Ingredients

1 C. dried morel
1 C. boiling water
2 C. all-purpose flour
salt
2 large eggs, beaten with
1/4 C. water
1 1/2 lbs Idaho potatoes, chunks

1/2 C. warm milk
1/4 C. sour cream
2 tbsp parmesan cheese
1 tbsp unsalted butter
ground pepper
vegetable oil
celery leaves

Directions

1. Get a heatproof bowl. Place in it the morels and cover them with hot water. Let them sit for 22 min.
2. Gently rub them with your hands then drain them and finely chop them.
3. Get a large mixing bowl: Mix in it the flour with 1/2 tsp of salt, eggs and 1/4 C. of water.
4. Place the dough on a floured surface and knead it until it becomes soft for 4 min. Cover it with a wet kitchen towel and let it rest for 32 min.
5. Bring a large salted pot of water to a boil. Cook in it the potato until they become soft. Drain them and mash them.
6. Get a large mixing bowl: Mix in it the mashed potato with milk, sour cream, parmesan, butter, morels, a pinch of salt and pepper. Place it aside to cool down.
7. Divide the dough into pieces. Flatten one piece of dough on a floured surface until it becomes 1/4 inch thick.
8. Use a 9 inches cookie cutter to cut it into circles. Repeat the process with the remaining dough.
9. Divide the filling between the dough circles and place them on one half of the circles.
10. Pull the other side of the dough over the filling and press the edges to seal them with a fork.
11. Bring a large salted pot of water to a boil. Place in it the pierogies gently and cook them for 1 to 2 min.
12. Preheat the grill and grease it.
13. Get a large mixing bowl: Toss in it the pierogies with some vegetable oil.
14. Place the pierogies on the grill and cook them for 2 to 3 min on each side. Serve them warm with your favorite dip.
15. Enjoy.

SWISS BEEF
Pierogies

Prep Time: 10 mins
Total Time: 25 mins

Servings per Recipe: 4
Calories	262.7
Fat	20.6g
Cholesterol	59.3mg
Sodium	790.0mg
Carbohydrates	6.2g
Protein	13.3g

Ingredients
16 oz. frozen pierogi
4 oz. deli corned beef, sliced thin and chopped
1 C. sauerkraut, drained well
1/3 C. thousand island dressing
4 oz. Swiss cheese, shredded

Directions
1. Before you do anything, preheat the oven to 425 F. Grease a casserole dish with some butter.
2. Cook the pierogies by following the instructions on the package.
3. Place the pierogies in the greased casserole. Top them with the corned beef, sauerkraut, dressing and end with the Swiss cheese.
4. Place the casserole in the oven and cook it for 12 min. Allow it to rest for 5 min. Serve it hot.
5. Enjoy.

Cabbage
Cream Pierogies

Prep Time: 30 mins
Total Time: 36 mins

Servings per Recipe: 1
Calories	679.2
Fat	29.5g
Cholesterol	110.3mg
Sodium	298.8mg
Carbohydrates	88.4g
Protein	21.7g

Ingredients
10 lbs green cabbage, chopped
2 cream cheese
1/4 C. unsalted butter
salt and black pepper
1 egg, beaten
1 C. milk
1 C. water

3 tbsp sour cream
4 1/2-5 C. flour

Directions
1. Slice the cabbage into 4 pieces. Place them in a steamer and cover them. Let them cook for 25 to 35 min.
2. Shred the cabbage and place it in kitchen towel then press it to remove the water from it.
3. Get a food processor: Place in it the shredded cabbage and pulse it several times until it becomes finely minced.
4. Mix in the butter with cream cheese, a pinch of salt and pepper until they become smooth.
5. Get a large mixing bowl: Combine in it the egg, milk, water, and sour cream. Mix in the flour with a pinch of salt until you get a dough.
6. Place the dough on a floured surface and cover it with a wet kitchen towel. Let it rest for 12 min.
7. Slice the dough into 4 portions and flatten them on a floured surface until they become 1/16 thick.
8. Use a 3 inches cookie cutter to cut the dough into circles. Place 2 tbsp of the cabbage filling at one side of the dough circle.
9. Pull the other side over the filling and press it with a fork to seal the edges. Repeat the process with the remaining dough and filling.
10. Bring a large salted pot of water to a boil. Cook in it the pierogies in batches until they float on top for about 4 to 6 min.
11. Drizzle over them some melted butter then serve them with your favorite toppings.
12. Enjoy.

TUESDAY'S
Pierogies

Prep Time: 20 mins
Total Time: 50 mins

Servings per Recipe: 12
Calories	338.0
Fat	21.8g
Cholesterol	86.5mg
Sodium	158.9mg
Carbohydrates	29.6g
Protein	6.5g

Ingredients
1 lb egg noodles
1 C. butter
salt
pepper
1 large sweet onion, finely chopped
1 (7 1/4 oz) boxes instant mashed potatoes
with four cheeses

2 2/3 C. water
1 1/3 C. milk
4 tbsp butter

Directions
1. Before you do anything, preheat the oven to 350 F. Grease a casserole dish with some butter.
2. Cook the noodles by following the instructions on the package until it become dente.
3. Get a large mixing bowl: Mix in it the mashed potato with water, milk, 4 tbsp of butter, a pinch of salt and pepper.
4. Place a large pan over medium heat. Melt in it 1 C. of butter. Add the onion and cook it for 8 to 10 min.
5. Place half the noodles in the bottom of the greased dish. Top it with 1/2 of the onion and all of the mashed potato.
6. Cover it with the remaining onion followed by the noodles. Place the dish in the oven and cook it for 32 min. Serve it hot.
7. Enjoy.

Pierogies
Stir Fry

🥣 Prep Time: 20 mins
🕐 Total Time: 35 mins

Servings per Recipe: 14
Calories   414.5
Fat   29.9g
Cholesterol   106.7mg
Sodium   267.9mg
Carbohydrates   5.7g
Protein   30.2g

Ingredients
1 tbsp vegetable oil
1 lb ground beef
1/2 C. chopped onion
1 packages frozen potato pierogi, thawed
1 packages frozen broccoli, florets, thawed
salt and pepper
1 C. shredded cheddar cheese

Directions
1. Place a large pan over medium heat: Heat the oil in it. Sauté in it the onion with beef and a pinch of salt for 6 min.
2. Stir in the pierogies and cook them for an extra 6 min. Mix in the broccoli with cheese, a pinch of salt and pepper.
3. Put on the lid and let them cook for 4 min. serve your pierogies skillet hot.
4. Enjoy.

CLASSIC
Homemade Pierogies Dough

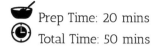

Prep Time: 20 mins
Total Time: 50 mins

Servings per Recipe: 1
Calories   20.2
Fat   0.2g
Cholesterol   8.8mg
Sodium   39.3mg
Carbohydrates   3.6g
Protein   0.7g

Ingredients
1 C. all-purpose flour
3/4 C. cake flour
2 large eggs
3/4 tsp salt
1/4 C. water

Directions
1. Get a large mixing bowl: Mix in it all the ingredients well.
2. Place the dough on a floured surface. Knead it for 9 min while adding more flour if it is too sticky.
3. Cover the dough with a wet towel and place it aside to rest for 32 min.
4. Enjoy.

Cheddar
Pierogies and Chicken Bake

Prep Time: 20 mins
Total Time: 40 mins

Servings per Recipe: 4
Calories   338.6
Fat   23.4g
Cholesterol   83.7mg
Sodium   734.3mg
Carbohydrates   7.8g
Protein   23.9g

Ingredients
2 lbs of Mrs. T's potato & cheddar
pierogies
1/2 large onion
2 frozen boneless chicken breasts
2 C. spinach
1 tbsp butter
10 1/2 oz. cream of mushroom soup

1 C. of shredded cheddar cheese
1 pinch salt & pepper

Directions
1. Prepare the pierogies by following the instructions on the package.
2. Before you do anything, preheat the oven to 350 F. Grease a baking dish with some butter or a cooking spray.
3. Place a large pan over medium heat: Heat in it the butter. Add the onion and cook it for 4 min. Stir in the chicken and with a pinch of salt and pepper.
4. Cook them for 6 to 8 min. add the spinach and cook them for an extra 2 min.
5. Stir in the mushroom soup with pierogies, a pinch of salt and pepper. Pour the mixture it the greased dish.
6. Sprinkle the cheese on top then bake the pierogies casserole in the oven for 22 min. serve it hot.
7. Get a large mixing bowl:
8. Enjoy.

CLASSIC
Chicken Pierogi Stew

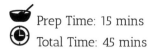

Prep Time: 15 mins
Total Time: 45 mins

Servings per Recipe: 4
Calories	317.5
Fat	8.4g
Cholesterol	111.4mg
Sodium	839.6mg
Carbohydrates	14.9g
Protein	43.1g

Ingredients
28 small frozen pierogi
1 tbsp vegetable oil
1 1/2 lbs boneless skinless chicken breasts, cut into 1/2 inch pieces
1/4 C. finely chopped onion
1/2 tsp minced garlic
1/4 C. all-purpose flour

3 C. chopped fresh spinach
1 (14 oz) cans nonfat chicken broth
2 C. skim milk
1/4 tsp salt
1/4 tsp white pepper
1/8 tsp nutmeg

Directions
1. Bring a large salted pot of water to a boil. Cook in it the pierogies for 4 min.
2. Place a large pot over medium heat. Heat the oil in it. Cook in it the garlic with onion and chicken for 6 min.
3. Mix in the flour and cook them for an extra 2 min. Add the spinach with broth, milk, nutmeg, salt and pepper.
4. Cook them until they start boiling. Lower the heat and let the soup cook for 12 min while stirring it often.
5. Add the pierogies and cook them for 4 min. Serve your soup hot.
6. Enjoy.

Vegetarian
Pierogies Dough

🥣 Prep Time: 1 hr
🕐 Total Time: 1 hr 15 mins

Servings per Recipe: 4
Calories   347.9
Fat   14.2g
Cholesterol   0.0mg
Sodium   583.3mg
Carbohydrates   47.6g
Protein   6.4g

Ingredients
2 C. all-purpose flour
1/2 C. warm water
2 tbsp warm water
1/4 C. vegetable oil
1 tsp salt

Directions
1. Get a large mixing bowl: Combine it all the ingredients and mix them well.
2. Place the dough on a floured surface and knead it for 4 min.
3. Wrap it in a piece of plastic wrap and place it aside to rest for 35 min.
4. Enjoy.

CHEESY POTATO
Pierogi Casserole

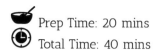 Prep Time: 20 mins

Total Time: 40 mins

Servings per Recipe: 6
Calories	620.9
Fat	39.8g
Cholesterol	109.8mg
Sodium	529.0mg
Carbohydrates	55.3g
Protein	13.4g

Ingredients
7 potatoes, cooked and mashed
2 large onions
6 - 8 pieces lasagna noodles
1 C. butter
1 C. cheese
1 (12 oz) cans evaporated milk

Directions
1. Before you do anything, preheat the oven to 350 F. Grease a baking dish with some butter.
2. Prepare the noodles by following the instructions on the package.
3. Place a large pan over medium heat: Heat in it the butter. Add the onion and cook it for 4 min.
4. Add to it the potato with cheese, a pinch of salt and pepper. Mix them well to make the filling.
5. Place 2 lasagna sheets in the baking dish. Pour over it 1/3 the potato mix followed by 1/3 of the cheese.
6. Repeat the process to make two extra layers. Pour the evaporated milk on top. Place the pan in the oven and cook it for 25 to 30 min.
7. Serve it hot with your favorite toppings.
8. Enjoy.

White Tuna
Pierogi Bake

Prep Time: 15 mins
Total Time: 1 hr 15 mins

Servings per Recipe: 6
Calories   155.6
Fat   6.0g
Cholesterol   31.7mg
Sodium   427.0mg
Carbohydrates   2.8g
Protein   21.1g

Ingredients

24 frozen potato and cheddar pierogies
2 tsp canola oil
2 celery ribs, chopped
1 medium onion, chopped
2 cans tuna in water, drained
2 cans cream of mushroom soup
1 tbsp reduced-fat mayonnaise

6 slices low-fat cheddar cheese

Directions

1. Before you do anything, preheat the oven to 350 F. Grease a baking pan with some butter.
2. Cook the pierogies by following the instructions on the package.
3. Place a large pan over medium heat: Heat the oil in it. Sauté in it the onion with celery for 6 min.
4. Mix in the tuna with mayonnaise, soup, a pinch of salt and pepper. Cook them for 2 min.
5. Place the pierogies in the greased pan. Spread the tuna mixture all over it. Place the pan in the oven and bake it for 46 min.
6. Top the tuna casserole with cheese and bake it for an extra 3 min. Serve it hot.
7. Enjoy.

SWEET BLUEBERRY
Pierogies with Berries Sauce

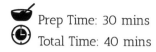 Prep Time: 30 mins

Total Time: 40 mins

Servings per Recipe: 1

Calories	90.5
Fat	1.7g
Cholesterol	9.9mg
Sodium	18.9mg
Carbohydrates	17.4g
Protein	1.6g

Ingredients

2 C. blueberries
1/2 C. granulated sugar
1 tbsp all-purpose flour
2 tbsp lemon juice
2 tbsp butter, melted
sour cream
2/3 C. granulated sugar
1 tbsp all-purpose flour

2 C. blueberries
3 C. all-purpose flour
1/2 tsp baking powder
1 egg
3/4 C. milk
2 tbsp butter, melted
cold water

Directions

1. To make the sauce:
2. Place a heavy saucepan over medium heat. Combine in it the blueberries, sugar and flour; add lemon juice and 1/4 C. water.
3. Cook them for 6 min over low heat until they become slightly thick.
4. To make the dough:
5. Get a large mixing bowl: Mix in it the flour with baking powder, egg, milk and butter. Add tbsp of water to the mix until it is no longer dry.
6. Place the dough on a floured surface and knead it for 4 min. Cover it with a kitchen towel and let it rest for 12 min.
7. Place the dough on a floured surface and roll it until it becomes 1/4 inch thick.
8. Use a 3 inches cookie cutter to cut the dough into circles.
9. To make the filling:
10. Get a mixing bowl: Mix in it the flour with sugar.
11. Place 1 tbsp of the sugar mix in on the side of 1 dough circle then top it with 1 tbsp of blueberries.
12. Pull the other side of dough over them then press the edges with a fork to seal them.
13. Repeat the process with the remaining dough and filling.
14. Bring a large salted pot of water to a boil. Place in it the pierogies and cook them until they float on top.
15. Drain the pierogies and serve them with the blueberries sauce.
16. Enjoy.

Pierogi Tortilla

🥣 Prep Time: 5 mins
🕐 Total Time: 10 mins

Servings per Recipe: 1
Calories	530.8
Fat	28.5g
Cholesterol	36.1mg
Sodium	931.4mg
Carbohydrates	52.6g
Protein	17.3g

Ingredients

1 small potato, thinly sliced
1 flour tortilla
1 tbsp crushed red pepper flakes
1/4 C. shredded Monterey Jack cheese
1/4 C. shredded Cheddar cheese
2 1/4 tsp Italian dressing
2 tsp olive oil

1 tsp basil
salt
pepper
salsa
sour cream
guacamole

Directions

1. Place a large pan over medium heat: Heat the oil in it.
2. Add to it the potato slices with basil, a pinch of salt and pepper. Cook them for 4 to 6 min until they become soft.
3. Drain them and place them aside. Lay the tortilla in the hot pan.
4. Get a large mixing bowl: Mix in it the shredded cheese.
5. Sprinkle it over the tortilla then top it with the cooked potato, red peppers, Italian seasoning, a pinch of salt and pepper.
6. Fold the tortilla gently in half then serve it hot right away.
7. Enjoy.

RED
Pierogies Skillet

Prep Time: 15 mins
Total Time: 30 mins

Servings per Recipe: 4
Calories   190.3
Fat   7.9 g
Cholesterol   11.5mg
Sodium   175.3mg
Carbohydrates   26.0g
Protein   5.1g

Ingredients
3 - 4 slices turkey bacon
12 - 16 pierogi, frozen
2 small carrots, sliced thinly
1 large russet potato, sliced thinly
1 medium yellow onion, diced
1 medium red bell pepper, diced
2 C. red cabbage, coarsely chopped
1 garlic clove, peeled and minced

oil, for frying
salt and black pepper, to taste
sour cream, for garnish

Directions
1. Place a large pan over medium heat: Fry in it the bacon until it becomes crisp. Drain it and place it aside.
2. Discard the bacon drippings. Heat 2 tbsp of oil in the same pan.
3. Cook in it the carrots with potato, pierogies, a pinch of salt and pepper for 12 min.
4. Stir in the bell pepper with onion and cook them for 6 to 8 min.
5. Add the garlic with cabbage and cook them for 3 to 4 min over low heat while stirring them often.
6. Mix in the bacon then serve your stir fry with some sour cream.
7. Enjoy.

Smoked
Apple Pierogies

🥣 Prep Time: 5 mins

🕐 Total Time: 35 mins

Servings per Recipe: 4

Calories	422.5
Fat	35.6g
Cholesterol	69.3mg
Sodium	942.9mg
Carbohydrates	11.2g
Protein	14.2g

Ingredients

1 tbsp olive oil
1 medium sweet onion, diced
1 large apples, diced
3 garlic cloves, minced
3/4 tsp dried thyme leaves
1 lb smoked beef sausage, sliced
1 lb potato and cheese pierogies

Directions

1. Prepare the pierogies by following the instructions on the package.
2. Place a large pan over medium heat: Heat the oil in it. Sauté in it the onion for 3 min.
3. Stir in the apple and cook them for another 3 min. Mix in the garlic with thyme, sausage, a pinch of salt and pepper.
4. Cook them for 4 min. Stir in the pierogies and cook them for 6 min while stirring them often.
5. Serve your apple pierogies skillet right away.
6. Enjoy.

DUMPLING
Pizza

Prep Time: 20 mins
Total Time: 40 mins

Servings per Recipe: 8

Calories	473.9
Fat	35.2g
Cholesterol	103.9mg
Sodium	943.0mg
Carbohydrates	17.1g
Protein	22.4g

Ingredients
2 prepared pizza crust, unbaked
3 C. mashed potatoes
1 large onion, peeled and diced
1/2 C. butter
8 oz. cheddar cheese, grated
8 oz. provolone cheese, grated
8 oz. mozzarella cheese, grated

Directions
1. Before you do anything, preheat the oven to 400 F. Grease a pizza pan with a cooking spray.
2. Place a large pan over medium heat: Heat the butter in it.
3. Add the onion and cook it for 6 min. Mix in the cheese with potato, a pinch of salt and pepper.
4. Spread the cheese and potato mixture in the pan. Lay over it the cheese slices. Cook them in the oven for 3 to 5 min.
5. Serve your pizza right away.
6. Enjoy.

Thursday's Dinner Casserole

Prep Time: 15 mins
Total Time: 45 mins

Servings per Recipe: 4
Calories	277.4
Fat	5.3g
Cholesterol	17.0mg
Sodium	650.2mg
Carbohydrates	43.1g
Protein	17.0g

Ingredients

1 1/2 C. cauliflower, diced
1 1/2 C. mashed potatoes
2 C. frozen broccoli florets
2 C. peas
2 chicken bouillon cubes
2 tbsp garlic, minced
1 tsp horseradish

1 tsp cayenne pepper
1 onion, diced
1 C. nonfat sour cream
1/2 C. parmesan cheese
salt and pepper
6 oz. wide egg noodles

Directions

1. Before you do anything, preheat the oven to 350 F. Grease a casserole dish with some butter.
2. Prepare the noodles by following the instructions on the package.
3. Get a large mixing bowl: Mix in it the veggies with horseradish, bouillon cubes, cayenne pepper, sour cream, half of the cheese, a pinch of salt and pepper.
4. Lay half of the noodles in the baking dish. Pour the veggies mix all over it.
5. Top it with the remaining lasagna noodles and cheese. Place the casserole in the oven and bake it for 32 min. Serve it hot.
6. Enjoy.

ELIZABETH'S
Pierogi

Prep Time: 20 mins
Total Time: 50 mins

Servings per Recipe: 4
Calories	584.2
Fat	40.4g
Cholesterol	121.9mg
Sodium	623.6mg
Carbohydrates	31.9g
Protein	24.5g

Ingredients
1 packages pizza dough
1 medium onion
4 tbsp butter
1/4 C. milk
12 oz. shredded cheddar cheese
4 -6 medium baking potatoes, cooked and
mashed

Directions
1. Before you do anything, preheat the oven to 350 F.
2. Get a large mixing bowl: Mix in it the mashed potato with milk, 8 oz. of cheese, a pinch of salt and pepper.
3. Place a large pan over medium heat: Heat in it the butter. Add the onion and cook it for 5 min.
4. Add the potato mix and toss them to coat.
5. Flatten the dough and place it on a lined up baking sheet. Top it with the potato mix followed by the rest of the cheese.
6. Place the pizza in the oven and bake it for 12 to 16 min or until it is done.
7. Serve it hot.
8. Enjoy.

Classic Sharpe
Pierogies' Potato Filling

Prep Time: 5 mins
Total Time: 5 mins

Servings per Recipe: 6
Calories   555.8
Fat   26.7g
Cholesterol   85.4mg
Sodium   1383.5mg
Carbohydrates   54.0g
Protein   24.6g

Ingredients
4 lbs mashed potatoes
1 lb shredded cheddar cheese
salt and pepper

Directions
1. Get a large mixing bowl: Combine in it all the ingredients well.
2. Enjoy.

IDAHO'S
Pierogies

Prep Time: 1 hr 30 mins
Total Time: 1 hr 35 mins

Servings per Recipe: 8
Calories	937.6
Fat	51.6g
Cholesterol	220.9mg
Sodium	1092.8mg
Carbohydrates	81.8g
Protein	37.5g

Ingredients
5 lbs Idaho potatoes, cooked and peeled
1 1/2 lbs sharp cheddar cheese, shredded
1/2 lb Velveeta cheese, thinly sliced
1 medium sweet onion, diced
Lawry's Seasoned Salt
pepper
1/4 lb butter
2 1/4 C. pre-sifted flour

3 medium eggs, beaten
2 tbsp sour cream
2 tbsp butter
milk

Directions
1. To make the filling:
2. Place a large pan over medium heat: Heat in it the butter. Add the onion and cook it for 5 min.
3. Stir in the cheese with potato, a pinch of salt and pepper. Mix them well.
4. Put on the lid and let them cool down.
5. To make the dough:
6. Get a large mixing bowl: Combine in it the eggs, butter and sour cream. Mix in the flour with a pinch of salt until you get a dough.
7. Place the dough on a floured surface and cover it with a wet kitchen towel. Let it rest for 12 min.
8. Slice the dough into 4 portions and flatten them on a floured surface until they become 1/16 thick.
9. Use a 3 inches cookie cutter to cut the dough into circles. Place 2 tbsp of the potato mixture at one side of the dough circle.
10. Pull the other side over the filling and press it with a fork to seal the edges. Repeat the process with the remaining dough and filling.
11. Bring a large salted pot of water to a boil. Cook in it the pierogies in batches until they float on top for about 4 to 6 min.
12. Drizzle over them some melted butter then serve them with your favorite toppings.
13. Enjoy.

Double
Stuffed Beef
Pierogies

🥣 Prep Time: 2 hr
🕐 Total Time: 2 hr 30 mins

Servings per Recipe: 8
Calories   599.3
Fat   20.3g
Cholesterol   264.7mg
Sodium   600.9mg
Carbohydrates   70.2g
Protein   31.0g

Ingredients

5 C. flour
6 egg yolks
3 eggs
1/8 tsp salt
3/4 C. water
1 C. cottage cheese
1 C. mashed potato
1 tbsp onion, chopped
1/8 tsp salt, pepper
1 1/2 C. cottage cheese
1/4 tsp vanilla

1 egg yolk
1 tbsp margarine, melted
1/2 tsp salt
1 1/2 tbsp sugar
1 lb ground beef
1 onion
1 tbsp margarine
1 tbsp flour
1/2 tsp dill
1/8 tsp salt, pepper

Directions

1. To make the meat filling:
2. Place a large pan over medium heat: Heat in it the margarine. Sauté in it the onion for 3 min.
3. Stir in the beef with a pinch of salt and pepper. Cook them for 6 min. Discard the excess fat.
4. Add the dill with flour and cook them for an extra 3 min. Place it aside to cool down.
5. To make the cottage cheese filling:
6. Get a large mixing bowl: Combine in it the sugar with cottage cheese, vanilla, margarine egg yolk and salt. Place it aside until ready to use.
7. To make the potato filling:
8. Get a large mixing bowl: Mix in it the cottage cheese with potato, onion, a pinch of salt and pepper. Place it aside until ready to use.
9. To make the dough:

10. Get a large mixing bowl: Combine in it the eggs and flour with a pinch of salt until you get a dough.
11. Place the dough on a floured surface and divide it into 3 portions.
12. Flatten them on a floured surface until they become 1/16 thick.
13. Use a 3 inches cookie cutter to cut the dough into circles. Place 2 tbsp of the filling you desire at one side of the dough circle.
14. Pull the other side over the filling and press it with a fork to seal the edges. Repeat the process with the remaining dough and filling.
15. Bring a large salted pot of water to a boil. Cook in it the pierogies in batches until they float on top for about 4 to 6 min.
16. Drizzle over them some melted butter then serve them with your favorite toppings.
17. Enjoy.

Pierogi
Poppers

🥣 Prep Time: 30 mins
🕐 Total Time: 45 mins

Servings per Recipe: 40
Calories   49.3
Fat   3.6g
Cholesterol   9.0mg
Sodium   96.8mg
Carbohydrates   3.5g
Protein   0.7g

Ingredients

1/2 C. onion, chopped
1/4 C. butter
8 oz. fresh mushrooms, finely chopped
3/4 tsp salt
1/4 tsp black pepper

1 hard-boiled egg yolk, chopped
8 oz. packages pie crust mix, crumpled
1/2 C. sour cream

Directions

1. Before you do anything, preheat the oven to 400 F.
2. Place a large pan over medium heat: Heat in it the butter. Add the onion and cook it for 4 min.
3. Stir in the mushroom and cook them for 4 min. Mix in the egg yolk with a pinch of salt and pepper. Turn off the heat.
4. Get a large mixing bowl: Mix in it the pier crust with sour cream until you get a smooth dough.
5. Combine in it the egg, milk, water, and sour cream. Mix in the flour with a pinch of salt until you get a dough.
6. Place the dough on a floured surface flatten it on a floured surface until it becomes thin.
7. Use a 3 inches cookie cutter to cut the dough into circles. Place 2 tbsp of the cabbage filling at one side of the dough circle.
8. Pull the other side over the filling and press it with a fork to seal the edges. Repeat the process with the remaining dough and filling.
9. Place the pierogies on a lined up cookie sheet. Place it in the oven and cook them for 16 to 19 min.
10. Serve them with your favorite dipping sauce.
11. Enjoy.

CREAMY
Sauerkraut Pierogies Casserole

Prep Time: 15 mins
Total Time: 1 hr 25 mins

Servings per Recipe: 6
Calories	537.4
Fat	20.3g
Cholesterol	25.7mg
Sodium	1625.3mg
Carbohydrates	71.0g
Protein	17.8g

Ingredients
1 lb pasta , farfalle
1/2 lb bacon, diced
1 large onion, chopped
8 oz. mushrooms, sliced
1 - 2 clove garlic, minced
1 cans sauerkraut, drained and rinsed
2 cans mushroom soup
1 - 2 bay leaf

Directions
1. Before you do anything, preheat the oven to 350 F.

2. Prepare the noodles by following the instructions on the package.

3. Place a large pan over medium heat: Cook in it the bacon until it become crunchy. Drain it and place it aside.

4. Stir the onion with mushroom, garlic and a pinch of salt into the pan. Cook them for 6 min.

5. Stir in the soup with sauerkraut and bay leaves. Cook them for 12 min over low heat.

6. Stir in the noodles with bacon. Pour the mixture into the casserole. Cook it in the oven for 35 to 46 min.

7. Once the time is up, discard the bay leaves then serve your casserole right away.

8. Enjoy.

Farmers' Butter Pierogies

🥣 Prep Time: 30 mins
🕐 Total Time: 60 mins

Servings per Recipe: 4
Calories	642.3
Fat	28.2g
Cholesterol	238.8mg
Sodium	1402.7mg
Carbohydrates	67.6g
Protein	28.6g

Ingredients

1 1/2 lbs farmer cheese
4 egg yolks
2 egg whites
1 tsp salt
1 tsp pepper
1/2 onion, grated
2 tbsp sugar

1/4 tsp baking powder
2 C. flour
1/2 C. salted butter

Directions

1. Place a large salted pot of water over high heat and bring it to a boil.
2. Get a large mixing bowl: Combine in it all the ingredients well.
3. Place the dough on a floured surface. Flatten it until it becomes 1/2 inch thick logs.
4. Use a sharp knife to slice the dough logs and drop the pieces in the boiling water. Cook them for 5 to 7 min.
5. Place a large pan over medium heat. Melt in it the butter. Add the pierogies and cook them for 3 min. Serve them right away.
6. Enjoy.

VIDALIA POTATO
and Noodles Pierogi Bake

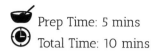

Prep Time: 5 mins
Total Time: 10 mins

Servings per Recipe: 4
Calories   579.0
Fat   28.8g
Cholesterol   122.8mg
Sodium   764.2mg
Carbohydrates   58.5g
Protein   21.7g

Ingredients

1/2 lb wide egg noodles, cooked
1/4 C. butter
1 1/2 C. mashed potatoes, prepared
5 slices American cheese
1/2 C. cheddar cheese, shredded
1/2 C. mozzarella cheese, shredded
1/4 large Vidalia onion, minced
2 garlic cloves, minced

salt and pepper, to taste

Directions

1. Before you do anything, preheat the oven to 350 F. Grease a casserole dish with a cooking spray.

2. Prepare the noodles by following the instructions on the package.

3. Place a large pan over medium heat: Heat in it the butter. Cook in it the garlic with onion, a pinch of salt and pepper.

4. Cook them for 5 min. Spread half of the lasagna sheets in the greased dish.

5. Spread over it half of the cheese followed by all the potato. Season them with some salt and pepper.

6. Cover it with the remaining pasta and cheese. Dot it with butter then bake it for 12 min.

7. Allow the lasagna casserole to rest for 5 min then serve it.

8. Enjoy.

Italian Style
Beef and Veggies Pierogies Skillet

🥣 Prep Time: 0 mins
🕐 Total Time: 30 mins

Servings per Recipe: 4
Calories	417.7
Fat	22.6g
Cholesterol	91.9mg
Sodium	889.9mg
Carbohydrates	23.5g
Protein	30.6g

Ingredients

1 lb ground beef
1/2 C. onion, chopped
1/4 C. all-purpose flour
1 cans beef broth
1 packages frozen cheese and potato pierogies, thawed
2 C. frozen mixed vegetables, thawed and
drained
1/2 tsp salt
1/2 tsp black pepper
1/2 tsp Italian seasoning
1/2 C. cheddar cheese, shredded

Directions

1. Place a large pan over medium heat: Brown in it the beef with onion for 8 min.
2. Discard the excess grease and reserve 3 tbsp of it only.
3. Add the flour to the beef mix and toss them to coat. Stir in the broth and cook them until they start boiling.
4. Let them cook for 2 to 3 min until the sauce thickens.
5. Add the seasonings with veggies and pierogies. Let them cook for 5 to 6 min. Top them with cheese then serve your skillet hot.
6. Enjoy.

WONTON CHEDDAR
Pierogies

🥣 Prep Time: 1 hr
🕐 Total Time: 1 hr 15 mins

Servings per Recipe: 12
Calories   208.3
Fat   11.6g
Cholesterol   32.8mg
Sodium   258.6mg
Carbohydrates   21.6g
Protein   4.5g

Ingredients
42 wonton wrappers
2 large baking potatoes, diced and cooked
1/2 C. cheddar cheese, grated
2 tbsp butter
salt and pepper
water
flour
1/2 C. butter

1/4 C. onion, very finely diced

Directions
1. Place a large pan over medium heat: Mash in it the cheese with beef, a pinch of salt and pepper.
2. Place a wonton paper on a working surface. Place 1 tsp of the potato mixture in the middle of it.
3. Brush the edges with some water then fold it in half. Press the edges to seal them and place the pierogies on a greased baking sheet.
4. Repeat the process with the remaining ingredients.
5. Bring a large salted pot of water to a boil. Cook in it the pierogies for 4 min.
6. Place a large skillet over medium heat. Heat in it the butter. Stir in the onion with a pinch of salt and cook them for 4 min.
7. Serve your pierogies warm with the onion sauce.
8. Enjoy.

Peanut Butter and Jam Pierogies

Prep Time: 30 mins
Total Time: 45 mins

Servings per Recipe: 15
Calories   153.5
Fat   5.9g
Cholesterol   32.3mg
Sodium   135.6mg
Carbohydrates   20.7g
Protein   4.7g

Ingredients

2 large eggs
1/2 tsp salt
2 C. flour
2 oz. cream cheese
water
7 -10 tbsp peanut butter
7 -10 tbsp jam, of choice

1/4 C. mini chocolate chip

Directions

1. Before you do anything, preheat the oven to 350 F.
2. Get a food processor: Mix in it the flour with salt, cream cheese and eggs until they become smooth.
3. Add the water and pulse them several times until they become smooth.
4. Wrap the dough with a piece of plastic wrap and let it rest for 22 min.
5. Get a small mixing bowl: Stir in it the peanut butter with your favorite jam.
6. Place the dough on a floured surface flatten it on a floured surface until it becomes thin.
7. Use a 5 inches cookie cutter to cut the dough into circles. Place 2 tbsp of the peanut butter mixture at one side of the dough circle.
8. Pull the other side over the filling and press it with a fork to seal the edges. Repeat the process with the remaining dough and filling.
9. Bring a large salted pot of water to a boil. Cook in it the pierogies for 3 to 5 min or until they float on top.
10. Serve them with your favorite dipping sauce.
11. Enjoy.

DOUBLE STUFFED
Pierogies

Prep Time: 30 mins
Total Time: 45 mins

Servings per Recipe: 4
Calories	550.1
Fat	16.7g
Cholesterol	166.8mg
Sodium	752.6mg
Carbohydrates	79.6g
Protein	19.5g

Ingredients

2 potatoes, cooked mashed
1 C. cottage cheese, drained
1 onion, minced and fried
1 egg yolk, beaten
1 tbsp butter, melted
1 tsp sugar
1/4 tsp salt
pepper, to taste

2 1/4 C. flour
1/2 tsp salt
2 tbsp butter
1 large egg
1 egg yolk
1/2 C. reduced-fat milk
2 tbsp sour cream
12 C. salt water

Directions

1. Get a large mixing bowl: Mix in it the mashed potato with cheese, onion egg yolk, butter, sugar and salt to make the filling.

2. Get a large mixing bowl: Mix in it all the dough ingredients until you get a smooth dough.

3. Cover it completely with kitchen towel and let it rest for 3 h.

4. Place the dough on a floured surface flatten it on a floured surface until it become thin.

5. Use a 3 inches cookie cutter to cut the dough into circles. Place 2 tbsp of the potato filling at one side of the dough circle.

6. Pull the other side over the filling and press it with a fork to seal the edges. Repeat the process with the remaining dough and filling.

7. Bring a large salted pot of water to a boil. Cook in it the pierogies in batches for 6 to 8 min.

8. Drain the pierogies then serve them with your favorite dipping sauce.

9. Enjoy.

Peppered Pierogies Casserole

🥣 Prep Time: 5 mins

🕐 Total Time: 30 mins

Servings per Recipe: 4
Calories	240.7
Fat	11.8g
Cholesterol	95.9mg
Sodium	348.3mg
Carbohydrates	2.1g
Protein	29.9g

Ingredients

1 packages frozen pierogi
1 lb boneless skinless chicken breast, strips
1/2 large sweet onion, thinly sliced
2 tbsp butter
1/4 tsp salt
1/8 tsp pepper
1/2 C. shredded cheddar cheese

Directions

1. Prepare the pierogies by following the instructions on the package.
2. Place a large pan over medium heat: Heat in it the butter. Add the chicken with onion, a pinch of salt and pepper.
3. Cook them for 6 min. Drain them and place them aside.
4. Stir the pierogies in the same pan and cook them until they become golden brown.
5. Stir in back the chicken mixture then top it with cheese. Put on the lid and let it cook for 6 min.
6. Serve your Chicken pierogies skillet warm with your favorite toppings.
7. Enjoy.

CRAZY SAUSAGE
and Milk Pierogies

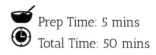

Prep Time: 5 mins
Total Time: 50 mins

Servings per Recipe: 6
Calories	252.9
Fat	17.0g
Cholesterol	70.9mg
Sodium	966.2mg
Carbohydrates	2.8g
Protein	21.4g

Ingredients
2 1/2 lb frozen potato pierogi
1 cans cream soup, mushroom or celery
1 cans milk
2 C. cooked beef sausage
2 C. cheddar cheese

Directions
1. Before you do anything, preheat the oven to 350 F. Grease a casserole dish.
2. Lay in it the pierogies then top them with the sausage, a pinch of salt and pepper.
3. Get a large mixing bowl: Whisk in it the milk and soup. Pour the mixture all over the pierogies followed by cheese.
4. Place the casserole in the oven and let it cook for 46 min. Allow the casserole to sit for 5 min then serve it.
5. Enjoy.

Golden Cheddar
Cream Pierogies

🥣 Prep Time: 10 mins
🕐 Total Time: 20 mins

Servings per Recipe: 4
Calories	1893.6
Fat	91.6g
Cholesterol	689.5mg
Sodium	4017.0mg
Carbohydrates	203.1g
Protein	63.5g

Ingredients

6 C. flour
10 oz. sour cream
4 eggs
1 1/2 tbsp salt
1 1/2 tbsp baking powder
2 1/2 lbs potatoes, cooked and mashed
3/4 lb cheddar cheese, grated

1/4 C. melted butter
5 eggs, whites divided
1/2 C. butter
1 C. chopped onion

Directions

1. To make the filling:
2. Place a large pan over medium heat: Mix in it the potato with cheese, 4 eggs, egg yolk melted butter, a pinch of salt and pepper.
3. To make the dough:
4. Get a large mixing bowl: Mix in it the all the dough ingredients. Shape the mixture into a ball and place it on a floured surface.
5. Flatten the dough and use a C. or a cookie cutter to cut it into circles. Put 1 tbsp of the potato mix in the middle of a circle.
6. Brush the edges with some egg white then top it with another dough circle. Press the edges to seal them.
7. Repeat the process with the remaining dough and filling.
8. Bring a large salted pot of water to a boil. Cook in it the pierogies in batches for 4 to 6 min until they float on top.
9. Place a large pan over medium heat. Heat in it the butter until it melts. Cook in it the onion for 4 min.
10. Stir in the pierogies and cook them for an extra 2 to 3 min. Serve them hot with your favorite toppings.
11. Enjoy.

SOUR CREAM
Pierogies

Prep Time: 5 mins
Total Time: 2 hr

Servings per Recipe: 16
Calories	267.4
Fat	12.0g
Cholesterol	48.2mg
Sodium	197.1mg
Carbohydrates	28.5g
Protein	11.4g

Ingredients
2 C. flour
1 C. milk
1 egg
1/2 C. sour cream
2 1/2 lbs russet potatoes, cooked
1 lb cheddar cheese, Shredded
1 lb onion, Diced

Directions
1. Get a large mixing bowl: Combine in the potato with cheese, onion, a pinch of salt and pepper.
2. Get a large mixing bowl: Mix in it the flour, milk, eggs, sour cream, and a pinch of salt.
3. Place the dough on a floured surface and flatten it until it becomes 1/8 inch thick.
4. Use a 2 inches cookie cutter to cut the dough into circles. Place 2 tbsp of the potato filling at one side of the dough circle.
5. Pull the other side over the filling and press it with a fork to seal the edges. Repeat the process with the remaining dough and filling.
6. Bring a large salted pot of water to a boil. Cook in it the pierogies in batches for 6 to 8 min.
7. Drain the pierogies then serve them with some chopped green onion and sour cream.
8. Enjoy.

How to Make
a Pierogi Gratin

🥣 Prep Time: 15 mins
🕐 Total Time: 40 mins

Servings per Recipe: 4
Calories	398.3
Fat	29.3g
Cholesterol	91.6mg
Sodium	791.8mg
Carbohydrates	14.3g
Protein	19.5g

Ingredients

1 (17 oz) boxes Mrs. T's potato and cheddar pierogies
2 tbsp butter
2 tbsp all-purpose flour
2 C. milk
1/2 tsp paprika
1/2 tsp salt

1/4 tsp ground black pepper
2 C. shredded sharp cheddar cheese
1/4 C. dried seasoned breadcrumbs
1 tbsp chopped fresh chives

Directions

1. Before you do anything, preheat the oven to 350 F. Grease a casserole dish with some butter.
2. Cook the pierogies by following the instructions on the package.
3. Place a pot over medium heat: Heat in it the butter. Mix in the flour well. Pour in the milk gradually while whisking them all the time.
4. Stir in the paprika with a salt and pepper. Turn off the heat and stir in the cheese until it melts to make the white sauce.
5. Stir the pierogies with the white sauce in the greased dish then spread them in an even layer. Place the dish in the oven and let it cook for 16 to 22 min.
6. Sprinkle the breadcrumbs on top then bake it for an extra 2 min.
7. Garnish your gratin with some chives then serve it hot.
8. Enjoy.

SPICY CRAB
Pierogies

Prep Time: 15 mins
Total Time: 30 mins

Servings per Recipe: 4
Calories	270.5
Fat	14.8g
Cholesterol	50.8mg
Sodium	731.5mg
Carbohydrates	18.9g
Protein	15.3g

Ingredients

8 oz. lump crabmeat, flaked
1 scallion, minced
1/4 C. minced red bell pepper
1/2 C. mayonnaise
1 tbsp Dijon mustard
1 tsp Old Bay Seasoning, divided
1/4 tsp Tabasco sauce
1/2 C. seasoned dry bread crumb, divided

1 (17 oz) boxes potato and cheddar pierogies
1 tbsp vegetable oil

Directions

1. Place a large pan over medium heat: Mix in it the crabmeat, scallion, red bell pepper, mayonnaise, mustard, 1/2 tsp Old Bay seasoning, Tabasco sauce, and 1/4 C. breadcrumbs.

2. Form the mix into the 4 patties. Roll them in the rest of the breadcrumbs and place them aside.

3. Season the pierogies with old bay seasoning, a pinch of salt and pepper.

4. Cook them in a large pan by following the instructions on the package. Drain them and place it aside.

5. Heat the oil in the same pan. Fry in it the crab patties for 2 to 3 min on each side. Serve them with your pierogies and your favorite toppings.

6. Enjoy.

Garlicky Semolina Dumpling Pierogies

🥣 Prep Time: 10 mins
🕐 Total Time: 15 mins

Servings per Recipe: 4
Calories   96 kcal
Fat   4.8 g
Carbohydrates   9.8g
Protein   3.3 g
Cholesterol   46 mg
Sodium   18 mg

Ingredients
5 tbsp semolina flour
1/4 tsp garlic powder
1/4 tsp Italian seasoning
1 egg
1 tbsp olive oil
1 pinch salt

Directions
1. Place a large pot over high heat. Fill it with water. Cook it until it starts boiling.
2. Get a mixing bowl: Mix in it the semolina flour, garlic powder, and Italian seasoning.
3. Get a large mixing bowl: Combine in it the egg, olive oil, and salt. Mix them well. Add the flour mix and mix them again until they make a smooth dough.
4. Spoon the dumplings into the hot water. Cook them until they rise to the top. Keep cooking them for 5 min. Serve them right away.
5. Enjoy.

ENJOY THE RECIPES?

KEEP ON COOKING
WITH 6 MORE FREE COOKBOOKS!

Visit our website and simply enter your email address to join the club and receive your 6 cookbooks.

http://booksumo.com/magnet

https://www.instagram.com/booksumopress/

https://www.facebook.com/booksumo/